MW00635737

A Friend Indeed: Help Those You Love When They Grieve

By

Amy Florian

Corgenius, Inc.

A Friend Indeed:
Help Those You Love When They Grieve
Amy Florian

Contributions by Ken Florian
Designed by Tanya Johnston

ISBN: 978-0-9896280-5-1
Library of Congress Control Number: 2017941101

Corgenius, Inc.
hello@corgenius.com
815 Woodlawn Street
Hoffman Estates, IL 60169

Ordering Information: Quantity sales. Special discounts are available on quantity purchases by corporations, associations, U.S. trade bookstores and wholesalers, and others. For details, contact the publisher at the address above.

www.Corgenius.com
Printed in the United States of America

First Edition

Contents

Dedication 11

Preface. 13

Background Information 17

    The Nature of Grief 17

    Grief Triggers 18

    Styles of Grieving. 22

    Disenfranchised Grief. 24

    Ambiguous Loss 25

    Anticipatory Grief 26

What *Not* to Say: Fifteen Phrases That Alienate
or Simply Aren't Helpful 29

What *to* Say: Twenty-Three Options That Comfort 39

Responding to the Initial Phone Call 51

Attending Services 55

Following Up After the Services. 63

    Invite the Story 63

    Tears and Tissues 66

    Helpful Strategies. 68

    Addressing Fears 71

    Putting Off Major Decisions. 73

    Don't Go Away 74

    Checking in on Your Level of Support 75

Emotional Differences between Divorce and Widowhood 79

Questions to Ask for Positive Transitions 83

Special Issues. 89

    Those Needing Professional Help 89

    When the Loss Involves Young Children 91

    Death by Suicide. 95

    Murder or Violent Death 99

Serious or Terminal Illness 103

    Background Information 103

    Facilitating Communication 105

    Watch for Fatigue When You Visit 106

    Concrete Help. 106

    Illness at Holiday Time 107

    Four Things That Matter Most. 108

    Hospice 111

When Your Pen Hovers Over the Page:
Condolence Cards and When to Send Them 115

    General Information and Schedule 115

    Immediately After a Death. 117

    A Monthly or Yearly Anniversary of a Death 123

    Holidays or Marker Days. 127

    Death of a Sibling. 130

    Death of a Child 131

    Death of a Parent 132

    Terminal Illness. 133

    Death by Suicide. 134

    Longer Texts: Letters for Various Intervals 136

Articles for Grieving Friends and Family 147

Anything and Everything, Except the Obvious. 148

Chasing after Closure 150

The Starting Point—Filling the Emptiness 152

Grieve with Hope. 154

How to Handle Your Fears after the Death of a Spouse 155

Keeping Busy. 159

The Changing Palette 161

The Fog of Grief: A Widow's Essay 163

The Greatest Gift 164

Twelve Steps for Healthy Grieving 166

Where Do I Turn? Recommended Books on Grief and Loss 169

General Grief. 170

Death of a Spouse. 175

Parental Death—for Adults 177

Child Death—for Parents 180

Sibling Death. 182

Books For and About Children or Teens 184

Divorce 188

Terminal Illness. 189

Dementia 191

Death by Suicide 194

Murder or Violence. 196

Pet Death 197

Conclusion. 201

Bibliography of Resources Used. 203

About the Author 205

Dedication

John Willenborg was an earthy Iowa farm boy whose easy laugh and generosity of heart endeared him to everyone he met. Life was simple for John. It was defined by love—for people, animals, God, the land, and most especially for me, whom he loved with his entire being. That love deepened as we lived through two difficult miscarriages, and it burst with joy when our long-awaited baby boy was born.

A mere seven months later, tragedy swept the joy out of my life. John was killed in a car accident, leaving me a twenty-five-year-old widow with an infant son. Unfathomable grief overwhelmed me, yet I knew I had to heal: Carl no longer had a father, so he'd better have a mother. Tossed by unpredictable waves of emotion, needing to redefine my purpose, identity, dreams, and very existence, I grasped for whatever resources I could find. Ever so slowly, I began to grow, heal, and gain wisdom forged in the crucible of pain. In the process, I found myself instinctually reaching out to others in grief, teaching them what I knew while continually learning more from them. John's love and his death reshaped the boundaries of my life and set me on a path I never could have anticipated.

Several years later, I met Ken, a highly intelligent, extremely well-read, deeply curious, and selflessly giving man with a profound compassion for those who suffer. Our journeys were not the same, yet threads of our experiences intertwined, informing and broadening the tapestry. Grappling with the implications of John's life and death for our relationship as a couple further defined and informed my perspective. In the meantime, Carl bonded with Ken and in fact began to call him "Dad" as soon as we announced our engagement.

I began doing more bereavement work, teaching sessions and helping to found a support group for widowed people. Ken encouraged my return to graduate school to combine my expanding body of on-the-ground knowledge with research and insights from psychology, neuroscience, and thanatology. He proudly framed my master's diploma and my first paycheck for an article. He cheered when I was hired to teach graduate classes. He challenged me when my reasoning was weak, shared material from his own reading, and promoted my personal and professional growth.

I now teach people across the globe how to support people they work with, serve, and/or love in times of transition, loss, and grief. We constantly receive e-mails, phone calls, letters, and texts thanking us for making a distinct difference in people's personal and professional lives.

Without John and without Ken, I would not be here, and this book would not be in your hands. To the men who so lavishly loved and supported me, I dedicate this book. May it bring you knowledge, competence, skill, and healing.

Amy Florian

Preface

Information You Need

When people you care about are grieving and in pain, do you stumble over timeworn phrases and unintentionally alienate or offend them? Or can you effectively walk them through the toughest times of their lives?

Most of us aren't very good at grief support, because we've never been taught. Instead, we often rely on what we've picked up from others along the way, inadvertently perpetuating mistakes. You need fresh knowledge from an expert, keen insights that expand your perspective, and practical applications that have a profound impact on your relationships.

That is why *A Friend Indeed* exists. Here, you receive information that's difficult to get elsewhere. These skills, grounded in solid research and tested with grieving people, equip you to be a true friend in a time of need. You can be there for those you love in ways others can't, because they've never been taught.

Easy to Navigate

Every chapter in this reference guide is concise and to the point, with pertinent examples and a little bit of the background research that undergirds the skills. It is perfect for when you need answers fast.

Educational information you can use is first on the agenda. Then later chapters contain text you can write in condolence cards and letters, articles you can give to friends and family members, and books to recommend or give to those in need of them.

Kindly Give Us Feedback

As you learn and apply these skills, please share with us your stories and your feedback. We will regularly update and revise this guide, further tailoring it to the needs of our readers.

Don't hesitate to contact us with questions or any additional needs you have. E-mail us at hello@corgenius.com or call us at 847-882-3491. We are here to help you.

We wish you all the best as you seek to be a true comfort to your friends in need.

Background Information

The Nature of Grief

We rightly associate grief with death because it is such a well-known cause. Indeed, surviving the death of a loved one serves as the most frequent example used in this guidebook. Yet it is vitally important to recognize that grief is an adaptive response to loss of any kind.

Grief occurs whenever an attachment is broken. Grief is triggered whenever you must leave behind someone, something, a function, a way of life, a dream, or anything else you've become attached to and do not want to live without. It strikes whenever one chapter is ending and another begins. It encompasses the "in-between" space when you learn to let go of what can no longer be, accommodate your life to that loss, and build a different future. Grief is the hallway between the room you must leave and the room that awaits.

Grief is neither an illness nor a pathological condition. It is an expected and normal process that allows you to maintain connections to what you lost while you simultaneously assimilate, accommodate, and go forward with life. Resolving grief does not mean you forget. Instead, grief helps you make sense of the past, create a memory out of all you've had, and move into a new, hope-filled future enriched by the memories.

In the midst of it, though, the grief process is wrought with pain, paradox, and tension—things we all prefer to avoid. We don't want to face the pain, the loneliness, the wordless cry, or the void that can never be filled in the same way again. In my initial grief, I often used the example of a blowtorch burning in my gut. Sometimes it was dialed up to high, sometimes it ebbed, but it was ever-present throughout my days and nights. We want to do anything we can to get away from it.

Unfortunately, running away doesn't work. Suppressing, denying, or ignoring grief does not make it vanish. Unresolved grief festers within and, like a volcano's molten lava, it pushes its way through to the surface, sometimes in ways we least expect. When we deny or ignore grief, we can give ourselves headaches, backaches, and stomachaches. Grief can spew into emotional outlets, especially anger, impatience, and disproportionate reactions to something else that happens in life. Repressed grief can manifest as clinical depression. Tragically, unresolved grief can cripple a person who is never fully happy and joyful again because there is too much hidden hurt, risk, and fear.

On the other hand, those who have the courage to face the pain, give expression to the experience, resolve the grief, and heal can emerge from the experience better, happier, and healthier, more tolerant of others, wiser, and more appreciative of life and all it holds. No teacher is as adept as the grief process if we are willing to learn.

When someone you love is grieving, then, your job is not to cheer them up, make them happy, "fix" it, or make it go away. You can't do that anyway. Your job is to companion them, to offer your strength to join with theirs as they struggle through. You offer compassion, a listening ear, and unfailing support.

Grief is hard work. So is grief support. Hopefully, this book will make it a little easier.

Grief Triggers

Because loss is ubiquitous throughout the life cycle, the people you care about are grieving more frequently than you think. Herbert Anderson and Kenneth Mitchell (in the book *All Our Losses, All Our Griefs*) list six types of loss or transition that trigger grief. They note that most transitions involve more than one of these intertwining losses. Each individual loss may be sudden (natural disaster) or gradual (Lou Gehrig's disease), total (divorce) or partial (distancing of a once cherished friendship), and temporary (wearing a cast for six weeks) or permanent (amputation).

You can use knowledge of these grief triggers to help people name their losses. When we name a reality, we can more easily cope with it. You may have noticed, for instance, that when you await the results of diagnostic tests, the anguish comes from not knowing what is wrong and wondering whether you are crazy. When you finally get the diagnosis, even if it is not what you had hoped or you face a tough road ahead, at least you have a name for it and you know what you're dealing with.

So when you understand the many triggers of grief that constitute any one loss, you can say to your loved ones, "Of course you're sad! Look at everything you've lost. Look at the number of grief triggers that are involved here [and name the triggers]. You're not crazy; you're just grieving over many things. Your reaction is normal." This alone can be tremendously comforting.

The six types of grief-triggering loss:

1. **Material: loss of a physical object, personal and/or sentimental possession, or familiar surroundings**
   - A treasured possession is broken, lost, or stolen.
   - A home burns down or is damaged/destroyed by a force of nature.
   - A car is totaled.
   - Money is lost in a market collapse, fraud, failed business venture, or gambling spree.
   - A family moves to a new home and leaves the old one behind.
   - Someone has to move into an assisted living community or skilled nursing facility.
   - Loss of data and contact records when a phone is stolen or a hard drive crashes.

2. **Relationship: partial or complete loss of a human or animal relationship**
   - Death of a family member, friend, or business colleague.
   - Divorce or separation.
   - Dissolution of a business partnership.
   - Cooling or distancing of a valued friendship.
   - Death of a pet.
   - Betrayal or infidelity.
   - Change in social circle or network.

3. **Intrapsychic: loss of a dream, whether the focus of the dream is oneself or others**
   - Infertility.

- Marriage breakup.
- Parenting a child with disabilities whose age-mates begin doing things the child will never do.
- Unfulfilled goals for life, career, or avocation.
- Loss of plans and hopes for a future with a person who dies.
- A failed business venture or attempt at entrepreneurship.

4. **Functional: temporary or permanent loss of a physical, cognitive, or mental capability**

- Losses associated with aging: arthritis, eyesight, hearing, energy levels, or ability to do the things one used to do.
- Partial or total paralysis of parts of the body.
- Illnesses such as ALS, Parkinson's, or dementia that progressively rob function.
- Loss of driving privileges.
- Injury or illness that affects the brain and/or mental capacity.
- Joint replacement that places permanent limits on some functions.
- Temporary loss of ability following surgery, accidents, etc.

5. **Role: loss of one's customary identity or "place" in a family structure, work organization, faith center, or other setting**

- A promotion to or demotion from a position.
- A formerly married spouse becomes a single parent through death or divorce.
- An adult child must care for a formerly independent parent.
- Parents become empty nesters, or empty nesters take in their grown child.
- A stay-at-home parent goes to work or vice versa.
- A working person fully or partially retires from the workforce.
- A student graduates and moves into the full-time workforce.
- A natural caregiver becomes a care receiver.
- A breadwinner can no longer hold a job or is down-sized.
- A business owner sells the business or takes on a partner.

6. **Routines: loss of the familiar structure of one's life**

- Taking on a job that involves a very different amount of travel.
- Becoming a parent with all the interruptions to sleep, activities, and freedom.

- Adjusting to regular visits to the hospital, nursing home, or other locations.
- Retirement.
- Entering physical therapy, chemotherapy, rehab, or any treatment requiring a series of set appointments.
- Moving to a nursing home or other facility with scheduled meals and activities.
- Enrolling in evening or weekend classes in addition to one's job.
- Adjusting to changes when the "social calendar" spouse is absent through divorce, death, or dementia.
- Renegotiating responsibilities in a marriage or partnership.

Many researchers add:

7. **Systemic: loss of faith in an entire system**
- Experiencing the reality that healthcare delivery is not as coordinated, efficient, and compassionate as it ought to be.
- Realizing the legal system doesn't always deliver justice.
- Losing faith in the political system or workings of government.
- Feeling betrayed by business in general or by one's place of employment.
- Failing to receive the aid or assistance assumed to be due.
- The shattering of assumptions about how life works or "should" work (children should outlive their parents; if you work hard you will be rewarded; etc.).
- Experiencing betrayal or doubts about the foundations of one's faith, church, pastors, or spiritual beliefs.
- Losing confidence in an institution such as marriage.

It may be surprising to note that even positive transitions trigger grief, because every time you move to something positive, you leave good things behind. Retiring, for instance, means leaving behind status, role, everyday routine, reason for getting out of bed in the morning, and daily interactions with colleagues. Most new parents grieve over the lack of sleep, the inability to be spontaneous and run their own lives, and the increased weight of responsibility that parenting entails.

There is a validated study called the Holmes-Rahe Social Readjustment Rating Scale or, in shorthand, the Holmes-Rahe Stress Scale. It assigns numbers to various life transitions based on the stress level caused and the likelihood that such stress will result in actual physical illness. Three of the top ten stress-inducing life events on the scale are typically understood as positive transitions! (Those three are marriage, marital reconciliation, and retirement.) Also in the top twenty-five are pregnancy, changing to a different line of work, and outstanding personal achievement.

So in your own life and with others, recognize that every transition involves grief, because every transition, no matter whether the end result is good or bad, entails leaving something behind and breaking attachments. In almost every instance, there are some things we are relieved about or happy for and, at the same time, things we are sad about or miss.

Regardless of the transition, grief will be deeper and more persistent when there are multiple triggers. During divorce, for instance, every grief trigger is involved except functional loss. When a family member has a severe illness requiring hospitalization and/or long-term care, all of the grief triggers may be involved. Therefore, be aware of the factors at work for each transition your loved ones face, so you can name their experience and support them through it.

The principles of grief support discussed in this reference guide apply to all types of losses. With variations to allow for the nature and depth of the loss, you can ask the same type of questions of a bereaved parent that you'd ask someone whose father has dementia. You demonstrate compassion to a person whose house burned down with the same principles that guide your response to one whose business failed.

Learn and practice effective grief support skills to make a positive difference through each of the many and varied transitions of life.

Styles of Grieving

Conventional wisdom suggests that men grieve differently than women. But that is not necessarily true. Grief correlates more to style than to gender. In fact, if you prejudge how people will grieve based on their gender, you risk alienating them.

The following two styles of grieving were developed through the research of prominent psychologists Kenneth Doka and Terry Martin and reported in their book *Grieving Beyond Gender: Understanding the Ways Men and Women Mourn.*

1. Intuitive grievers

Intuitives experience grief more in their heart than their head, as a deep feeling that they must express and talk through. They process and tell their story repeatedly. They are more likely to keep a journal. They seek out support groups and other people in similar situations. The types of questions they are most likely to ask include the following:

"Who can emotionally understand and advise me?"
"Who can I talk to about my feelings?"
"How can I process this so I don't hurt so much?"
"What books can I read so I know I am not alone?"

2. Instrumental grievers

Instrumentals experience grief more in their head than their heart, as a physical, cognitive, or behavioral phenomenon. They want to face facts and take actions. They try to remain objective and analyze the experience. They are more likely to go it alone or go to an individual grief coach or counselor than to seek support groups, and are wary of emotions that might cloud their judgment. They are most likely to ask questions like the following:

"What concrete actions do I need to take to get through this?"
"How can I manage my grief and move on?"
"How can I keep my emotions in check so they don't hold me back?"
"What can I read to help me learn how to cope?"

It is statistically true and probably consonant with your experience that more women lean to the intuitive side of the spectrum, while more men are instrumentals. Nevertheless, make no assumptions. Some women are strongly instrumental, and some men fall squarely in the intuitive camp. For example, there was a male lawyer who came to the widowed support group I facilitate. Although you'd expect him to be an instrumental griever, he is an intuitive. He cried through the meeting, and said with a wry smile that since his wife died, he buys far less toilet paper and far more tissues. I've also worked with women who rarely cry and are strongly instrumental in their approach.

Like most personality traits, the distribution of grieving styles falls along a continuum. Few people are entirely one or the other; most function as a blend of both. (I am near the middle, with some strong intuitive tendencies and some strong instrumental tendencies.) Adding to the complexity, many people function as intuitive grievers with some losses but grieve instrumentally with others. Or professionals who naturally lean to the intuitive side may feel pressure to function in the office as instrumentals.

Finally, current research is focusing on the effects of Myers-Briggs personality types and how they affect grieving styles. This research is confirming that how we cope with grief is not as dependent on male-female differences as we have assumed in the past.

Think about your own experience and try to determine where you land on the spectrum. Then use that awareness along with information in this book to recognize and develop fluency across styles, allowing people to grieve in their own ways without judgment even when they grieve differently than you.

Disenfranchised Grief

"Disenfranchised grief" is the psychological term first used by Kenneth Doka in 1989 for losses that we poorly support or understand. It reflects the reality that not every loss receives adequate validation in our society, largely because we value particular types of relationships more than others. People regularly report, for instance, that when a beloved pet died, would-be comforters "consoled" them by minimizing their grief, saying, "At least it was only a cat."

When society at large doesn't value a relationship, we grant less credence to the loss experience, deny the possibility of deep grief, and may exclude the griever from even rudimentary support. Employment policies sometimes reinforce the disenfranchisement. For instance, employees are allowed bereavement leave for the death of an immediate family member but not for the death of a lifelong best friend or a cousin who is emotionally closer to them than any sibling. Instead of receiving the support and empathy they need, bereaved people in these situations feel isolated and misunderstood.

Examples of disenfranchised losses include:

- Death of a pet
- Death of an ex-spouse

- Death or disability of a partner in a committed but non-marital relationship
- Miscarriage or stillbirth
- Infertility
- Death of an adult sibling (grief support and concern tends to concentrate on parents and children of the deceased rather than the brothers and sisters)
- Death of an elderly or infirm family member
- Material loss by fire or natural disaster (the "we-still-have-each-other" syndrome, in which gratitude for people negates legitimate sorrow over the loss of home or treasured possessions)
- Loss of an online friend or long-term gaming companion
- Death of the person to whom a loved one donated organs
- Children or others who are not allowed to attend services or who are not supported in their bereavement

The list goes on. Your task is to take your loved one's every grief seriously, including those that seem trivial to you. Always ask people what it's like for them and listen with compassion, acknowledging any disenfranchisement. They need you to notice, validate, and seek to understand their experience, especially when so many others don't.

Ambiguous Loss

"Ambiguous loss," a term first coined by psychologist Pauline Boss, refers to incomplete and ongoing loss with no definitive closure, or any loss that is impossible to resolve.

Most ambiguous losses fall into two categories:

1. A person is physically absent but psychologically present: for example, a soldier missing in action, a kidnapped child who can't be found, or a family member who either abandoned the family or ran away. Ambiguous loss is also a factor when a loved one is declared dead but the body cannot be recovered, leaving family members with nagging questions about whether a death has actually occurred.

   Families in these situations maintain hope that their loved ones will return, although over time that hope becomes increasingly tenuous. Eventually, as the practical implications of the person's absence press in, the family is forced to adjust to life as if the person died. In the midst of uncertainty over their loved one's fate, they live with constant tension over how much to let go versus how much to cling to hope for return. This deeply stressful, long-term process is often poorly supported.

2. A person is physically present but psychologically absent: for example, a family member who lives in the home but is emotionally distant, a loved one who exists in a persistent vegetative state, or a beloved person living with dementia, significant brain trauma, or severe disability.

In these cases, the physical body is still there and alive, needing care, and usually dependent on the family. At the same time, family members mourn the inch-by-inch diminishment of the whole person who once inhabited the body. Their loved one may be growing gradually more distant or seem to be already gone from them. This is particularly the case if the person is in an unrecoverable coma, or if he or she has reached the point of no longer recognizing familiar people and remembering their visits.

Since the loved one is present in body only, family members often anguish over decisions about how often to visit or what it means when they do. They may be facing significant medical costs, confusing decisions about treatment, and struggles with adjusting to life in light of the ambiguity. Be prepared to support them through the complexities of this difficult and painful situation.

Anticipatory Grief

When an unexpected or sudden loss occurs, survivors are thrown into a crucible as their lives are immediately and unalterably changed. Sometimes, though, a loss comes slowly over time, as when a person slides gradually but inexorably toward his or her final breath. Grief does not wait for the actual event. People also grieve in anticipation of a loss they know is coming.

Examples:

• As high school seniors prepare to move out of the house or go away to college, their parents, already grappling with the childhood that is no more, anticipate their child's absence and the loss of a relationship quality that is only possible when people live together. Parental grief is usually deeper than that of their children, since parents anticipate diminishment of their home lives, while children anticipate the excitement and adventure of widening their world.

- When parents decide to downsize their home, the entire family has to leave behind memories that sing from every wall and activities that occurred in every room. They grieve the impending loss of place since someone else will move in and this will never be "home" to them again. They may find themselves frequently sitting in favorite places, taking in cherished views, remembering and grieving. Even when the move makes logical sense, it is fraught with emotion.

- As parents age—and especially when they encounter increasing health problems—both they and their children anticipate inevitable outcomes and become more concretely aware of death. They mourn each time a function, ability, or aspect of physical appearance slips away, each additional medical issue, and each bit of evidence that the parents are gradually and inevitably approaching the end of their lives.

- The dying trajectory of a terminally ill loved one may take days, weeks, or months, but everyone knows how it will end. Grief begins with the diagnosis, and then increases dramatically as death becomes ever more imminent and people begin saying goodbye.

In any of these cases, and particularly when a loved one is dying, it takes awareness and courage for family members to resist the urge to protect against pain by detaching too soon. Everyone benefits if they can stay engaged and continue to share their joys and sadness with each other. (See the section on terminal illness for more information about how to stay present during the dying process.)

In all cases of anticipatory grief, help those you care about to name the reality. Let them know it is normal to grieve both present and impending losses. Invite their stories, and listen as they share their experience with you, especially as it changes over time. Be there for them in ways that others aren't.

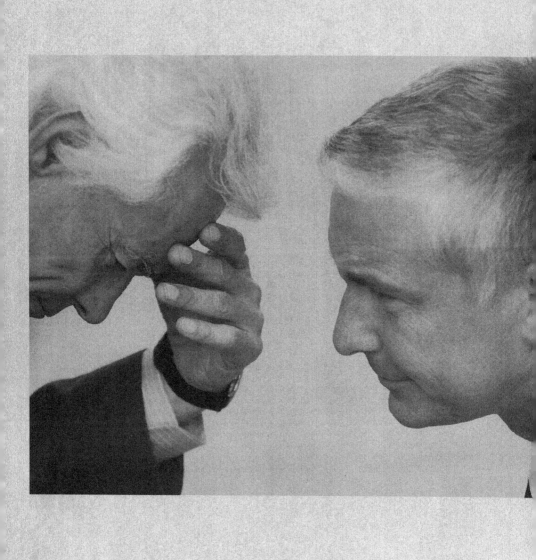

What *Not* to Say: Fifteen Phrases That Alienate or Simply Aren't Helpful

The Nature of Grief

Because we are never taught what to say when someone is grieving, we pick up what we can by listening to others. Unfortunately, that perpetuates mistakes. To break the cycle, avoid the following list. Some are general caveats. Others apply to specific situations.

You will no doubt be surprised that some of these are unwise; you've heard and said them for years. Yet, when you employ these phrases, your impact will be neutral at best. At worst, you risk unintentionally alienating grieving people when they are already in pain.

1. "I'm so sorry."

There are a number of reasons to eliminate this universal phrase from your repertoire.

- It is indeed a universal phrase. Everyone says, "I'm so sorry," whether they truly mean it or not. Even for those who mean it, no matter how compassionately they say those words, by the time grieving survivors hear it hundreds of times it loses its impact. You want to be heard and to make a difference. This is not the best way to do it.

- For most people, their first and most resonant context for the words "I'm so sorry" is as an apology for wrongdoing. That usage is so ingrained in us from a young age that the phrase triggers the internal psychological reaction of an apology. People are good at suppressing inappropriate responses, yet many mourners feel an urge to reply, "That's OK. It wasn't your fault." I've even heard support group attendees say, "I wish people would quit apologizing for my husband's death. They didn't do it." Not everyone will react that way, but why risk it?

- The phrase says something about how sad you feel but says nothing about them. It may even prompt grievers to feel they need to comfort you instead of the other way around. Bereaved people, in fact, get weary of having to comfort and educate others when they are so in need themselves.

- Finally and most importantly, it is a conversation-stopper because there is no good or comfortable reply. "Thank you" is the most common response, but that doesn't feel quite right if you think about it. Many survivors resist the impulse to answer, "So am I," or, as those in support groups tell me they wish they could say, "Not half as sorry as I am!" If a mourner does say, "Thank you," or otherwise respond, then what happens? There is no opening for dialogue, it's awkward and uncomfortable, and the interaction tends to stop there.

For all these reasons, "I'm so sorry" is not the best thing to say. It can and does express concern when you say it with sincere compassion, and in surveys, mourners will sometimes say it was one of the most comforting things people said to them. However, when pressed further, it becomes apparent that mourners find "I'm so sorry" to be comforting only because no one said anything better. You can offer greater, more genuine comfort that distinguishes you from the crowd and truly makes a difference.

2. "You have my sympathy."

This phrase, like "I'm so sorry," is so omnipresent that it loses its impact. At least this time there is a logical response. You "gave" the grieving person something, so it makes sense for them to reply, "Thank you." Unfortunately, you didn't give anything except the knowledge that you care, a sentiment you can more effectively express in other ways.

3. "I know how you feel."

If you want to alienate and anger grieving people immediately, tell them you know how they feel, because you are always wrong. Even if you've had a similar loss, you can't assume others approach it or experience it in the same way. An entire spectrum of factors determine a person's grief experience, including personality, prior experiences of loss, strength of support networks, grieving style, culture, faith traditions, particular relationship to the deceased, and more. The honest reality is that you don't know how they feel, and grievers unanimously resent it when you say you do.

4. "I can't imagine what you're going through."

Actually, we have pretty active imaginations, and we can at least partly fathom how awful an experience can be. What this phrase implies instead is, "I don't want to imagine what you're going through because it's too painful to put myself in your place." Thus it can actually cause grieving people to feel even more isolated, like no one is capable of understanding their experience and therefore cannot support them through it. You don't want to tell people you know how they feel; also avoid telling them you don't *want* to know how they feel or that you couldn't relate to it if you did.

5. "Time heals all wounds."

This well-worn phrase isn't true. Time puts distance between you and the event, but it doesn't heal anything. It is what you do with the time that heals. When you tell bereaved people time will heal them, you imply that grief follows a knowable timetable and you unconsciously encourage them to repress or deny their grief in the hope it will simply go away. This is the worst thing they can do if they want to reclaim joy in life. Grief does not go away if we don't face it, express it, resolve it, and heal.

6. "At least . . ." or "You should be grateful that . . ."

All mourners have things for which they are grateful. At the same time, they are deeply sad over what can no longer be (i.e. they may be glad that the loved one is no longer suffering yet sad because they will never hear that delightful laugh again). When you concentrate on only one side of the equation, you clearly telegraph that you don't understand their swirling mix of emotions. Your words minimize their pain. They learn you are just like everyone else—much more comfortable with the relieved and "happy" side of the experience and intent on cheering them up. From that point on, they suspect they can't be honest with you about their pain and sadness. Remember that your job is not to cheer them up; your job is to companion them wherever they are.

7. "Call me any time."

Hundreds of people say this; few honestly mean it. Although their intentions are good, they do not actually want the grieving person to call any time, whether during the day or at midnight, nor to ask them for any little thing they might need. Unconsciously, the phrase may also be an excuse for would-be comforters to let themselves off the hook: "Well, I told him to call me if he needed anything. He's not calling me, so he must not need anything."

Even beyond these issues, no matter how sincerely you invite the call or how deeply you mean it, grieving people are not going to call you. Grief saps their energy and concentration, making it difficult to articulate questions or needs. They feel vulnerable when they have to ask someone for help. They fear becoming a burden and do not want to intrude or impose. They are aware that although their lives are a shambles, your life is normal, and they wonder how big their need has to be to justify interrupting your normal life to ask for something. They simply aren't going to pick up the phone. It ends up being a meaningless offer, so there is no good reason to say it in the first place.

8. *"You look good."*

This is particularly applicable to people who are seriously or terminally ill. Others constantly tell them how good they look, hoping it will boost their spirits. It doesn't, especially in cases where they objectively do not look so good, where seeing themselves in the mirror evokes tears and longing for the "old" self. They wonder what else you are not addressing honestly in your efforts to make them feel better. Even in those cases where they currently do look surprisingly good, they know it won't last and they wonder whether you will still be comfortable with them when they look terrible. Finally, as people become progressively more ill, exterior concerns pale in comparison to the reality of the disease and their impending death. They begin to let go of social norms and keeping up appearances. For all these reasons, it is better not to place any focus on outward looks.

9. *"There's nothing more that we can do for you."*

For those with serious or terminal illnesses, these words are depressing and ominous. They are also false. Even when there is nothing medically that can cure an illness, there is still so much that can be done for the person—by you, a hospice team, the family, and more. Everyone can be helped to live as fully as possible until they take their last breath. This is an immense source of hope; don't snuff it out!

10. *"He's in a better place," or "Everything happens for a reason," or any attempt to explain or justify the loss.*

Some pertinent cautions here:

- No explanation is sufficient to satisfy mourners or to justify their loss.

- We don't know the answers or the reasons, and grieving people do not want others to impose beliefs or rationalizations on them.

- Tragedy and loss quite frequently knock the foundations of religious and personal belief out from under people (at least temporarily), and they need freedom and permission to grapple with those issues over time.

- It can be risky to assure survivors their beloved is in a better place, particularly without full knowledge of the family "secrets" and back-story. Sometimes survivors are honestly not convinced of their loved one's present location. You risk unintentional alienation by your confident assurance of the deceased person's happiness.

- Even when people do believe their beloved is in heaven or has attained nirvana, at that moment it is hard to imagine a "better place" than right by their side on this earth. Some mourners want to reply, "He's in a better place, but I'm not!"

- Remember that every transition is a "both-and." Survivors have things they are happy about *and* things they grieve for, and you need to rec-ognize both sides of the equation. It is perfectly normal for people to simultaneously be happy for their loved ones, but sad for themselves. As is the case with "At least" statements, when you concentrate only on the happiness of the deceased without recognizing the grief of the survivor, mourners know you don't understand.

11. "Should"

It is common for people to tell grievers what they should feel, how they should act, when they should clean out the closet or take off the ring, how they should handle their grief, and more. These well-meaning "shoulds" come from the unconscious ignorance of people who don't understand or who are not in the bereaved family's shoes. Survivors learn to say, "Thank you" to all the unwanted advice, and some may try to comply in order to please those in their support circles, but they resent all of the unsolicited and oh-so-confidently proffered "advice."

12. "Be strong."

In our society, we are taught that a grieving person should always strive to "be strong," refusing to succumb to "weaknesses" like anger, sadness, or tears. The truth, however, is that although it takes a lot of energy to stuff down the grief, tears, and emotion, it takes real strength to let it all come up. We would rather not face the pain, the loneliness, and the void that will never be filled in the same way again. Grief is hard, courageous work, and it takes real strength. It is not the strong who don't cry; it's the strong who do.

Give those you care about permission to embrace the full range of their experience, both positive and negative, and have that experience honored and respected. That is the path to healing. (See additional information on crying and repressed grief in the section Tears and Tissues.)

13. "How are you?"

It is difficult for a grieving person to accurately answer this query. Although they suppress the urge, they are often tempted to respond with, "How do you think I am? My child just died!" Additionally, it seems that although everyone they encounter asks this question, most of them don't really want to know. Finally, even if an inquirer seems sincere, grief is such a volatile process of ups and downs that mourners may feel differently from hour to hour, and certainly from day to day, making it difficult to answer accurately. Overall, it's easier for them to dismiss the question by saying, "Fine," than it is to respond with a painful but honest explanation that would actually contribute to their healing or that would open the door to dialogue. "How are you?" isn't helpful—to them or to you.

14. "Put it behind you and get on with life now."

Grieving people are confused and offended by suggestions that place their loved one firmly into a box marked "Past" or that imply the way to move ahead is to forget. Instinctively, it doesn't seem right, nor is it consistent with research on grief resolution. Rather than putting the past "behind" them, the path to healing involves creating a memory out of what can no longer be and *taking it with them into the future*. The goal is not to "get over" or forget it; the goal is to assimilate the memories and acclimate to the loss in order to "get on with life." We continue to honor and remember them for as long as we have breath.

15. Euphemisms

In our denial-prone society, we are afraid to use the actual words for death, illness, prognoses, and other "uncomfortable" transitions. We euphemize them beyond recognition as we dance around, add humor to, avoid, or try to soften the reality. While this may seem compassionate, it is counter-productive. The first step toward healing is facing and accepting the loss and its implications. When you use euphemisms, you participate in avoidance and let your friends and family members know that you are like everyone else—more comfortable with denial than with painful but healing truth.

Be particularly vigilant to avoid euphemisms around children because they are concrete thinkers. If you tell them Grandpa went to sleep, they might not sleep peacefully again. If you say the deceased went to heaven, they will wonder where heaven is located and why you can't just go visit them there. If you say their beloved aunt expired, they will wonder about their own expiration date. If you say someone was called home, they won't answer the phone. Children need honesty and information you can explain on their level, along with accurate words and explanations.

What *to* Say: Twenty-Three Options That Comfort

Now that you know what not to say, what do you say instead? Some of these twenty-three options are useful during any transition. For more situation-specific examples, you can often modify the language to suit other transitions or losses. You can also get ideas on what to say by reading the card texts in this book's chapter on writing condolence cards. Regardless of the situation, every one of these offers comfort, understanding, and compassion.

1. "How is it different?" Or "But what it is like for you?"

Instead of telling someone you know how they feel, this is your principle: Reference the fact that you have some experience or knowledge of a similar situation, establishing a common base of understanding, but then allow for their unique experience by asking a question.

Examples:

- "When my husband died in a car accident, I felt like I was walking around in a fog for over five months. Is it like that for you, or how is it different? What are you experiencing?"

- "When my dad died, Mom didn't know what to call herself anymore or what title to use on the return address of envelopes. Besides, she was the first person in their card group to be widowed, and now she feels like she doesn't fit into her social circle anymore. When people become single again, whether through death or divorce, they often struggle with issues like these—identity, losing friends, and more. Now that you are in that club, are these issues that you are struggling with, or how is it different? What is hard for you?"

- "I recently learned that grief can be like a roller coaster of up and down, back and forth, and it sometimes feels like you take three steps forward and two steps back. Is it like that for you, or what is your experience?"

- "A friend once told me that so many people try to help and they mean well, but because they don't know any better they end up saying and doing things that are hurtful. Has it been like that for you, or not? Is there something people have said to you that's been helpful, and are there other things that were not comforting or even caused you pain?"

> *2. "I bet you've had a lot of people tell you they can't imagine what this is like for you. If you could get into their imaginations, what would you tell them?" Or "I'm trying to imagine what this is like, but I've never been in your shoes. What can you tell me that will help me better understand?"*

This is an honest acknowledgment of the truth. It doesn't tell them you already know how they feel. It also addresses the other side of the coin: We have active imaginations that actually can envision the awful nature of this loss. So if you say, "I can't imagine what you feel," it isolates grieving friends and family, implying that you don't really want to know. Instead, admit your lack of firsthand knowledge but also your desire to better understand and support them. It opens the door so they can tell you their story, which is healing in itself. Then, given insight into their experience, you can more accurately imagine their reality and more capably companion them.

> *3. "I know your grief won't be over in a week, a month, or even a year. Keep putting one foot in front of the other. Keep breathing. This will take a long time, and I'll be here for you."*

Most people at the services will go home within a week and stop calling shortly thereafter. Let grieving friends and family know you won't go away, that you have understanding and patience with their grief, and that they can count on you for the long haul. When you say this, of course, make sure you live up to your promises! Keep checking in, calling, visiting, sending cards, and being willing to listen through the entire process of their grief.

> *4. "Healing doesn't mean 'getting over it' or forgetting. You heal by letting go and adjusting your life to the loss, while creating memories of what can no longer be and taking them with you into the future. In fact, the greatest testimony you can give to those you love is to live as fully as possible now, enriched by their memory. You carry the life, love, lessons, stories, and memories with you. You will never forget, and you wouldn't want to. [Name] will forever be part of you."*

This little nugget of education reassures grieving people that what they've heard from so many others is wrong. It brings relief when they realize they don't have to find a way to put their beloved in the past or forget. It acknowledges that although they do have to let go of the physical presence of the person, their beloved remains with them in memory and in the fiber of their being, and can enrich their lives in the future. Forgetting is not the goal.

There will never be a point of final closure, a time when grievers can say, "I will never miss her again. I will never cry again. I will never wonder what life would be like if he were still alive." For a significant loss, they will have "ambushes" or "grief bursts" for the rest of their lives. It may be triggered by something unexpected, as when someone who hasn't cried in years walks into a store, hears the person's favorite song playing on the store speakers, and bursts into tears. Alternatively, it may occur in conjunction with anticipated events, such as when the classmates of a deceased child graduate from college or when a daughter walks down the aisle without her father. This is normal and healthy. People gradually let go of the physical presence but not the love, the life, the memories, or the stories.

5. *"Grief is not linear or predictable. Expect a roller coaster."*

The grief process is not a linear progression where people gradually feel better every day until they are magically healed, nor does it move neatly through pre-ordained "stages." Instead, it is up and down, back and forth, and can often feel like three steps forward and two steps back. Your friends and family need reassurance that their recurring sad times and vacillating emotions are a normal and expected part of the healing process.

In fact, the sad times often arise precisely because survivors are healing, as the reality sinks in (both the reality of what happened, and the implications of what happened for their lives). And every time the reality strikes home again, whether it is a birthday, anniversary, the holidays with an empty chair, a child's age-mates accomplishing something their child never will, a phone call asking for the one who died, etc., it will trigger sadness and longing. Grieving people are sad over and over. They are happy over and over, too, and eventually the happy times prevail. Yet times of sadness are normal, particularly at first but also for a very long time to come.

6. *"I'll call you."*

Instead of asking a grieving person to call you when there is a need, take that burden on yourself and proactively call them. For close relationships, you may wish to set up a regularly scheduled time at which the phone will ring. Or every time you contact grieving friends, let them know when you'll call again. Or simply make it a habit to call on a regular basis. This way, mourners never have to wonder whether their questions are big enough to justify interrupting your day. They never have to muster up the energy and strength to call you. They know you will be there without them having to give it a second thought. This is refreshingly different from everyone else, and quite a relief!

7. *"I'd like to help. Would you rather I run some errands for you, babysit so you can get out by yourself for a while, take you out to lunch, help write or address thank-you notes, or do something else you need?"*

When you ask grieving people what you can do for them, they often cannot give you an answer. Perhaps their minds go blank due to the natural "fog" of grief, or, because they don't want to impose, they may be reluctant to ask without knowing what types of things you are actually willing to do. In any case, it puts the onus on the bereaved to formulate and state their needs.

Instead of making a generalized offer, list a few specific things. Grievers then know they can choose directly from your list or they can name a similar request with confidence that they aren't being burdensome or inappropriate. In some cases, it is advisable to simply do something. Organize a group of friends to provide meals to the family during a hospitalization, arrange for volunteers to get kids to their practices and activities while a newly-single parent figures out how to rearrange life, etc. Diving in to do what you know needs to be done, or offering concrete suggestions for what you can do, are protocols that ensure you will be helpful, while reinforcing that you understand more deeply than everyone else who simply asks, "What can I do?"

8. "You don't have to talk if you don't want to. I'm here for you anyway. I'll hold your hand if you want, sing to you, pray with you, hug you, or just sit together. I'm here for you all the time, not just when you feel like talking."

We tend to be terribly uncomfortable with silence. Yet sometimes there just are no words to say, or no words that need to be said. Whether you are visiting someone in the hospital/hospice, or seeing a grieving friend, let them know you aren't there to "cheer them up" and you won't leave when they run out of things to say. Sometimes, let silence say what words cannot.

9. "We don't understand why things like this happen."

Rather than attempting to explain away a loss, theologically or otherwise, simply admit the truth—we honestly don't know why things happen as they do. All we know for sure is that this did happen. It's always better to let people grapple with their own questions and doubts instead of offering a rationale that may not make sense to them or that may even alienate them. Invite them to tell you about it, and listen without judgment. Avoid giving answers, especially the standard platitudes that are easy to say but ultimately do not comfort.

10. "Death is not fair or logical, and it's always too soon when it's someone you love."

Death is unpredictable. It strikes young and old, fit and frail, healthy and seriously ill. It does not abide by rules of equity, and its only logic is the fact that everyone will die.

Death seems particularly unfair and illogical when it comes early in life. Yet even when a loved one's death follows old age or infirmity, survivors mourn and miss that person. People wish their eighty-eight-year-old Grandpa could have lived to be ninety-eight. When it is someone beloved, death is always too soon. Survivors are sad about the deaths, missing those who died and wishing they could have lived longer. Distinguish yourself from people who say, "You are so lucky he lived such a long life," or other familiar (but ultimately unhelpful) comfort phrases. Acknowledge the ambiguity of death and their love for the deceased.

11. Break the tension and invite dialogue when grievers tell you they are "fine."

"Fine" is the standard answer people give when they think you don't really want to know. Turn the word into an acronym, such as Frightened, Insecure, Neurotic, and Exhausted. Then add a little levity when people say they are "fine" by replying, "Ooh, you know what FINE means, don't you? It means frightened, insecure, neurotic, and exhausted. I'm not so sure that's a good thing." This will often elicit a chuckle. Then follow up by saying, "Besides, that's the standard answer people give when they think you don't really want to know. I honestly do want to know. I will always listen to the truth, even when it's hard. So would you like to tell me what's really going on?"

Use this whether people are actively grieving, stressed out, diagnosed with a terminal illness, or going through any transition. They may not wish to talk; always follow their lead and allow them to say no. But it's amazing how often they will smile, sigh with relief, and gratefully tell you what they are experiencing.

12. "I will do whatever I can to make this difficult process easier for you."

Grieving people can feel overwhelmed by complexity and often find it hard to concentrate on a paragraph in a book, much less a new future. This reassuring phrase—which can be said at countless points during the grief journey—admits your limitations while simultaneously acknowledging that your goal is to help make things easier and less complex. Then follow through with presence, frequent communication, and emotional support.

13. "It's normal to be relieved or grateful about some things and at the same time very sad about others. Most people bounce back and forth between the two. It's all normal; just allow whatever comes."

When you say something like this, you give permission to experience both sides of the grief equation. Instead of telling them to always look at the bright side, be positive, or be grateful, you accept them where they are and allow a level of authenticity that many others simply can't handle.

14. "Tell me more," or "What I hear you saying is . . . Is that accurate, or how would you explain it?"

First, simply invite mourners to keep talking. Then check in to make sure you understand what is being said. This lets them know that you are listening deeply and with great care. It also feeds you knowledge you need to offer your best support.

15. "This wouldn't be so hard if you didn't really love her.
Life can go on as usual when you lose something
unimportant, but never when you lose a treasure.
Your grief is a testament to your love, and there's no
reason to be ashamed or apologize for that."

Grieving people frequently berate themselves for not being "better" by now, especially with so many others telling them to put it behind them and get on with life. Reassure them their grief is a normal reaction to losing something precious. Validate the enormity of the loss. Allow the grief without shaming or judging. Give permission to feel, cry, and heal.

16. "It's hard when people say hurtful things, isn't it?
They mean well, and are doing their best to be com-
forting. They just don't know any better. They haven't
been taught, and they've never been in your shoes."

No one intends to be cruel or hurtful; they do the best they can. Yet grieving people are frequently offended, alienated, shocked, or cut to the core by another's words or actions. Help them be patient with the attempts, focusing instead on the underlying good-hearted intention. Many in the support groups tell me they get accustomed to simply saying, "Thank you for your concern," and then moving on.

You may also wish to follow up with a question: "What is one thing someone said to you that you did find comforting, and what is one thing that made you want to simply shake your head?" Not only does this let them know you understand their reality, it also gives you the opportunity to learn what this particular person finds comforting and annoying, so you are less likely to make mistakes yourself.

17. "Don't let anyone 'should' all over you."

Some people are ready to clean out the closet two weeks after the funeral (and by the way, these are likely to be instrumental grievers). Others cannot touch that closet for months. Both are normal. After a death or divorce, some people are ready to go out and date again fairly soon, while others cannot imagine that concept. Both are normal. Yet grieving people are so often told what they "should" feel, think, or do by those who believe they know better.

Tell mourners not to let anyone "should" all over them. (If you say this quickly, it may also get a chuckle!) Encourage them to trust their own instincts for what they are ready to do and when. In addition, since our instincts aren't 100% reliable, consider giving them a good book about grief, hopefully as closely matched to their situation as possible. (See the chapter on books for suggestions that you can give or recommend with confidence.) Then support and companion them as they follow their unique path to healing, taking care that you do not "should" on them either. Always remember to ask, not to tell, unless they request your opinion or advice.

18. Say the name.

Mourners want to know that others also remember their loved ones. They long to hear the name and share stories, even if it brings tears to their eyes. An old African tribal saying is pertinent here. It proclaims, "No one is ever truly dead from this earth until there is not a person left alive who speaks their name or tells their story."

Recall how we do this with our societal grief. On the yearly anniversary of 9/11, for example, we pause, tell the stories, and read every single name. We pledge never to forget, and we take actions to ensure the memories live on. Don't be afraid to say the name, in person or on a card. Keep the stories and memories alive, and help maintain the legacy of the one who died.

19. Say "died," "death," "cancer," "terminal illness," "died by suicide," "murder," etc.

An old proverb explains, "The beginning of wisdom is calling things by their right names." Using the proper words to describe what happened isn't nearly as harsh as people fear, and it is an honest recognition of reality. Some grievers fall in step with the rest of society and resist using accurate words like death, died, suicide, cancer, and so forth. Do not force them, but try not to follow suit. For instance, if someone says, "When Mom passed away...," you can say, "So when your mom died..." When you have the courage to accurately name what happened, you let mourners know they don't have to dance around it with you. This can be freeing for them and distinguishes you from all the others who avoid using the real words.

This is particularly important with children, who are such concrete and literal thinkers. Answer their questions at their level, but do so using the correct terminology.

20. "You're not crazy; you're just grieving. What you're saying/thinking/doing is normal for a grieving person."

Bereaved people frequently feel that they're going crazy, especially when they face significant loss or transition. The intense, all-encompassing, and unpredictable nature of grief is a shock. They want to be "over it," and are constantly told they should be. In fact, after the first few weeks, well-meaning people may suggest they need psychiatric medication. While it can be incredibly helpful for grieving people to utilize the services of a support group or grief coach, only a tiny percentage of people sink into diagnosable mental problems. Affirm and reassure your friends and family by normalizing their experience and letting them know they're OK.

21. "You are unlearning the expected presence of [name]."

We learn to expect the beloved one to be there as usual. The hardest times are when that expectation isn't met. For example, it takes a long time to "unlearn" that when you pick up the phone and dial that number, there's not going to be an answer on the other side. Out of habit, the bereaved may call out a loved one's name when they come home. They see another person of similar build and hair color walking down the street and, for just an instant, believe it's their beloved. If a pet died, they may unthinkingly make the familiar trek to the pet food aisle. Grieving people have to retrain their brains not to expect the familiar presence, and that takes time.

*22. "It's hard to let go. You want to go back to
normal. But you can't; that normal is gone.
Wherever this process leads you, I am here to help
you remember the old and build something new."*

Although some transitions occur by choice, in many cases grievers are dragged, kicking and screaming, into a club they never wanted to join. They want their old life back and yearn for what can no longer be. Reinforce for them that there is no way to go back. The only way out is forward. It doesn't mean you forget; it does mean it is necessary to accept the fact that although life can be wonderful and well worth living, it will never be the same again.

*23. "You still have a future. It will just be a very
different future than the one you planned."*

Not only do grieving people feel they've lost what they cherished from the past, but they also feel they've lost their future. Actually, what they've lost is their dream for a particular future, or their vision and plan for how the future was expected to unfold. Part of their task is to let go of those dreams and eventually build new ones. This is easier said than done, but when you reframe it in this hopeful way, you help them begin the gradual shift from looking backward and asking, "Why?" to looking forward and asking, "What now?"

More Ideas

In addition to these options, you can glean more ideas for what to say by reading through the suggested texts in the chapter on writing condolence cards as well as the longer letters. In addition to their use in cards, these words are appropriate on the phone, in a letter, in the office, or when running into a friend on the street.

When you use these skills and phrases, you let those you care about know you are truly listening in ways that most people don't. You help them heal. There is no more meaningful gift you can give.

Responding to
the Initial Phone Call

Perhaps you've experienced something tragic or difficult, and noticed that you keep thinking, "This isn't real. This is a nightmare. I'm going to wake up tomorrow and it's going to be gone." The more shocking, upsetting, or unexpected an event is, the longer it takes to wrap your brain around it. One primary way we make it real is to hear the words coming out of our own mouths, over and over again. In fact, one of the greatest needs grieving people have is to tell the story.

Keep this in mind throughout the grief process, and especially in the initial instance when you get the news.

Example: You answer the phone and your friend says, "I'm just calling to tell you that Jim died last night." As noted above, most people say "Oh, I'm so sorry!" But that gets you nowhere, and it ultimately is not supportive. Instead, say something like, "Oh my, what a shock! Would you like to tell me what happened, or how you found out, or who is with you now?" In other words, you invite the story, giving various options that allow your friend to answer in whatever way he or she chooses.

In most cases when you issue a compassionate invitation, grievers will begin telling the story, perhaps with disbelief, as they try to comprehend what happened. Just listen, and then ask questions based on what they convey.

If a death followed a long illness and was expected, you can shift your response to something like: "Well, we expected that it was coming, although it still feels like a bit of a shock to actually hear the words. So, who was with you at the end, or who is there now? Does it seem like a bit of a shock to you, does it seem peaceful, or what is it like?"

Perhaps, as sometimes happens, your friend says they don't have time to talk right now, or perhaps the story has been told and your friend needs to go. Offer concrete suggestions of assistance: "What do you have on your plate that I can help with? Can I make some phone calls for you? Would you like me to contact the funeral home or the church? Can I bring over a big urn of coffee? Or what else can I do to help?"

Responding in these ways ensures that your friend knows you care, provides a way to let the reality begin to take hold, and also opens a path of helpful actions you can take to be of real assistance.

Attending Services

If the grieving family is of a different cultural or faith tradition than yours, research that tradition ahead of time so you understand expectations and avoid unintentionally offending them.

That being said, recognize that gathering to mark a death runs deeply throughout human cultures. In some parts of the world and some ancient traditions, the purpose is aimed at those who die, to help them get to where they need to go (and to make sure they stay there rather than haunting the survivors). In most of the developed world, the focus is on those who continue to live.

The primary reason for these gatherings is to come together as a family, as friends and community, to remember three things: who we are, how we belong to each other, and how we will forever be different because this person has died. The gathering and the rituals or services that constitute it help us to join hearts, hands, and voices to celebrate the life, recognize the death, and begin the formal goodbye.

Whenever you know the person who died or you know a family member, make every effort to attend the services in order to help them accomplish these tasks. There's no substitute for personal presence to let them know you care, especially when you ensure that everything you say or do focuses on the grieving family members and their needs rather than on you. You are not there to pay your respects, do your duty, or make a required appearance. You are there to help remember and celebrate the person's life, acknowledge the void and what will be missed in the absence, and offer reassurance that the survivors are not alone as they say their goodbyes.

You will not fulfill that purpose by joining the others on the conveyor belt, going down the line saying, "I'm so sorry," or "You have my sympathy."

Follow these steps instead to offer real comfort in a situation where so many others fail to do so.

1. Mentally compile two or three stories and memories you can share.

If you knew the person well, this should be an easy task. If you didn't know the deceased person (for example, your friend's grandparent), read the obituary and search the internet or other sources to glean useful information. At the same time, take note of the family members listed in the obituary so you are prepared for who will likely be in attendance.

2. Practice ahead of time.

Role play is invaluable. Running through scenarios in your mind is infinitely less effective than saying the words aloud with another person. Enlist the help of a colleague, family member, or friend. Practice what you will say from the moment you extend your hand to the grieving person. You want the words to flow easily and naturally without conscious thought on your part. After role-playing, you can reinforce it by saying the words out loud to yourself as you drive to the gathering.

3. Greet your friend and the family warmly.

In most cases, increasing your physical connection has a comforting psychological effect, yet that is not the case for everyone. Your principle is to greet your friend and the family in the manner that seems natural, while always following their lead by being sensitive to body position, muscles stiffening up, or other non-verbal communication.

If you have a warm and affectionate relationship, go ahead and offer a hug, and don't let go until your friend does. If not or if you are unsure, take your friend's hand in both of yours, or shake your friend's hand while putting your other hand on the elbow or upper arm. Then lean slightly in, which gives them permission to close the physical distance between you or even to reach out for a one-armed hug or a full embrace. On the other hand, if your friend responds by stiffening or by stepping back, then you gently step back to allow more space and return both hands to the handshake.

4. Unless you are absolutely sure the person knows who you are, briefly introduce yourself.

Grieving people can't think clearly and if they don't know you well they may have a hard time placing you. Or perhaps your friend is the one who died, and you are greeting family members you rarely or never met. Remove any awkwardness by reminding them of your name and connection. Then go immediately to the following step.

5. Name the reality and offer comments focused on the grieving person.

"I came tonight because I care about you." If you know the person who died, you can add, "And I loved Karen."

"I was so shocked when I found out Al died. I just had to come and tell you how much I care and how much I will miss him."

"Helen's death was expected, and yet when people actually take their last breath, it's always a shock. I came because I know this is not easy for you, and I wanted to let you know I care."

6. Go on to give a story or memory.

"I've been thinking about Sharon a lot, and I realized that the memory I'll carry with me for the rest of my life is her big, infectious smile. So many times, I saw her walk into a room and start smiling. Soon, everyone else in the room was smiling too. She certainly knew how to make people happy. We are definitely going to miss that smile!"

"I never met your father, but I noticed how much work he did with the non-profit organization. I'm sure they are going to miss the unique contributions he made to their work."

"I'll never forget when Sheila told me her plans to surprise you for your fortieth wedding anniversary. What a grin she had on her face! She really loved you."

"Keith could be pretty gruff, and not everyone found it easy to work with him, but under that gruff exterior, he obviously really wanted to do the right thing. I appreciated that soft side of him, and it was clear to me how much he loved all of you."

7. Ask your friend for a story and start a dialogue.

"But you knew her so much better than me. Tell me, what do you hope people will remember about Carol?"

"But I never had the privilege of meeting your grandfather. Tell me a story about him that you hold close to your heart."

"Your dad told me he will always remember [memory] about your mom. But kids have a different perspective than the spouse. So tell me, what will you remember, or what do you wish others knew about her?"

"I saw the pictures on the table at the entrance. In one of them, all of you are dressed up in silly costumes and your brother is right there in front. What is the story behind that picture?"

Then listen intently with good eye contact, and ask other questions based on the answers. Keep the dialogue going as long as your friend or other family members remain engaged in the conversation.

Don't worry if there is a long line behind you. Your job is not line management! Besides, the family knows the next fifty people in line will just say, "I'm so sorry," or "You have my sympathy." They'd rather spend time sharing stories or memories with someone who cares. Remember, your purpose is to serve and comfort the family, and facilitating conversations like this will surely do so.

8. Don't be afraid to name both sides of the equation.

"Of course we're glad he's no longer suffering. No one wanted him to suffer. And yet, we're really going to miss that wacky sense of humor."

"You were incredibly fortunate to have her with you for so long and she did live well. Yet that makes it all the harder to be without her now. Death always comes too soon when it's someone you love."

"No matter what relief there may be or any other positive aspect of this, the world has a hole in it now that no one else will ever fill in quite the same way."

9. End with support.

When you notice your friend disengaging (such as looking at the people behind you, shifting weight from foot to foot, or tapping your hand nervously), simply glance at the line yourself and say something like, "There are a lot of other people who want to talk with you and honor Michael, so I won't take more of your time now. I know, though, that many of these people are going to go home in a few days or a week. Realizing what happened here and coping with this loss takes longer than that. So I am here for you for the long haul. I'll call next week just to check in, and I'll continue to do whatever I can to make this difficult situation just a little easier for you."

10. Talk to other family members if desired

Contrary to common belief, there is no requirement to talk with everyone at the services. You can go in and out of the line, talking to whomever you wish.

In situations where you've never met other family members but you would like to speak with them, you can seamlessly make the transition as you leave your friend's side. After offering your support, you can say, "Could you help me out here? I want to share some stories with your brothers and sisters, too, but I have never met them. Could you point them out to me?" The response will likely be, "Oh, of course. This is Tom, Kevin, and Susanne." You can even talk with the three of them together if you'd like, rather than going to each one individually.

As you talk with other family members, repeat steps 1 through 9 with slight modifications to fit the relationship. For instance, you might say, "I just told your dad that my fondest memory of your mom is her big, infectious smile. It was amazing how she could walk into a room and get everyone smiling. Your dad and I agreed that we will all miss that. Your dad also said he hopes people remember her for her beautiful flower gardens and the joy they brought to so many people. Yet kids often have a different perspective. Tell me, what do you hope people will remember most about your mom? Or what is a story you tell with each other that makes you smile?"

Continue in this manner until you've spoken with as many people as you choose. It never hurts to stay a while, and with these steps in mind, you always have something comforting to offer.

Overall, do you see how this process is so much more authentic and supportive than the same-old litany that predominates at services? You fill the grieving family's needs, and they remember you long after you're gone.

Flowers versus Donations, Cards, and Gifts

It is a common practice to send flowers to the funeral home. Reconsider that practice.

In some cases, flowers are not particularly welcome. Judaism and Islam, for instance, do not encourage flowers. Even if the services are Christian, in which flowers are omnipresent, you have better and more comforting ways to spend your money. In fact, the plethora of flowers creates a problem for the family, because they rarely know what to do with them. They feel responsible to take care of them, or they feel guilty that hundreds or thousands of dollars was spent on the arrangements.

Instead, create a more lasting legacy by using the money you would have spent on flowers to make a donation in memory of the one who died. In the obituary, increasing numbers of families request that in lieu of flowers, donations be made to a specified organization. In that case, honor their wishes. If an organization is not specified, donate to a non-profit whose mission intersects with the family or with the cause of death—for example, a cancer research organization, the hospice that served them, the church in which the deceased was active, etc.

Use any remaining money on cards, gifts, or flowers that you send later, throughout the first year and beyond. Gain suggestions for appropriate gifts and cards by reading through the texts for condolence cards, especially those for later in the year or on special days like birthdays, holidays, or anniversaries.

Following Up
After the Services

Invite the Story

Just as with the initial phone call, remember how important it is for grieving people to tell the story, and recognize that the need persists for a very long time. It can take weeks or months for the reality to sink in. If you ask good questions and really listen, you can help that to happen.

This is particularly important because, sadly, within days or weeks of a significant loss, few people listen to the story anymore. Instead, they start instructing grievers to "put it behind them and get on with life," or to "get over it." Wherever mourners go, there's a big white elephant in the room that everyone tries to avoid, ignore, or peek around. If you don't bring up the topic, you fit in with all the others who cannot name the reality. Although you may exchange pleasantries or even go out together, there will be an awkward and uncomfortable aspect of your encounter, and your grieving friend will go home feeling unsettled.

So whenever you interact with grieving people, consistently ask open-ended questions that invite their story, and then follow their lead. Open a door, issue an invitation, and then give them freedom to walk through the door or to close it. Most of the time, they will walk through the door and tell you the story because they are so hungry to talk to anyone who is willing to listen.

Even if your friends close the door by choosing not to talk at that particular time, the big white elephant disappears and the tenor of the entire encounter changes. You also give permission for them to reopen the door later because they know you are comfortable with their grief and willing to listen. You have nothing to lose by asking good questions.

The following are examples of some helpful questions that invite people to talk. In many cases, the answers they give provide you with valuable information so you can better support them through the entire grief process.

"What do you wish people knew about what you're going through?" *(Listen carefully to the answer because people will tell you what they wish you knew.)*

"How do you wish people would act around you?" *(You will learn how they wish you would act around them.)*

"Who are the most supportive people around you, and what are they doing to support you so well?" *(When you listen, you'll discover what this person considers to be helpful, so perhaps you can do some of those helpful things, too.)*

"In what ways has the reality sunk in, and in what ways does it still just seem unreal?" *(Continue to ask this question for months afterward because it takes a long time for the reality to fully hit—both the reality of what happened and the full implications what happened for their lives.)*

"What has surprised or shocked you about this experience?"

"For some people, evenings are the hardest. For others, it's the weekend, or just after waking up in the morning. When are the toughest times for you?" *(You may wish to specifically reach out, call, or visit during the toughest times.)*

"How do you handle the tough times, and what practices have you found to be most helpful?"

"What do you most need right now to help you get through?"

"Many people find that their friendship circle changes after a death or loss, particularly a divorce or after a child or spouse dies. Friends they thought would be there forever sometimes disappear, and others may appear that you don't expect. What is it like for you? Do you feel discomfort among your friends, or in what ways is your friendship circle changing?"

"The last time we talked, you said you felt *[like a strand of blown glass]*. Is that still true, or what has changed since then?"

"What kind of day has it been for you today?" Or "Is this an up day, a down day, or an all-over-the-place day?" (*This is better than "How are you?" because it encourages a different response than either "Fine" or "How do you think I am?"*)

"Your family members are grieving too. Which of them seem to be handling it in ways that are similar to you, and who grieves differently from you? Which, if any of them, are good talking companions for you?"

"Are there any people in your circle you're worried about, and if so, in what ways?"

"What kinds of things went swirling through your mind when you got the news?"

"Now that you're a bit down the road in this process, what advice would you give to other people who are newly grieving a similar loss?"

As you ask these questions and other similar ones, practice active listening. Lean toward your friends and keep good eye contact. Nod your head and encourage them with occasional affirmative phrases and sounds like, "Uh-huh," "I see," "That must have been hard," or "Tell me more about that."

When you're talking with more than one person, make a conscious effort to include everyone in the conversation. You can do this by looking directly at a person who has said little and say, "Shelley, not everyone has the same experience in these situations. Is your perspective like Tom's, or in what ways is it different for you?" Then continue looking at Shelley while she answers. If Tom interrupts, politely say, "Hold that thought for just a minute, Tom. Shelley, you were saying?"

When grieving people pause in the story, three effective skills invite them to continue. For illustration purposes, assume the person said, "When the doctor walked into the room, I could tell by the expression on her face that the news wasn't good."

1. Restate what was said but in question form. "So when you saw the expression on the doctor's face, you knew it wasn't good?" Then pause, and the person will pick it up from there.

2. Rephrase the words with added details. "So when you saw that expression on the doctor's face, you got scared and braced yourself?" Or "It sounds like the clue to brace yourself for bad news was written all over her face?"

3. Request more information. "What kinds of things went through your mind when you saw the doctor's expression?" Or "Was there anything else besides the doctor's facial expression that you found disconcerting?"

These queries lay a good foundation you can build on over time. Continue to ask these and other open-ended questions based on what your friend or family members tell you so you can continue to companion them effectively.

Tears and Tissues

Most of your friends and colleagues have grown up believing that crying is a sign of weakness. Tears are especially problematic for men in our death-denying society. Many of them are raised to deny emotions and never shed a tear.

Consequently, when people start to cry in the presence of others, they often apologize. Commonly, you will also hear, "I just have to be strong," which translates into, "I can't show my emotions or cry."

In this context, we inaccurately define the word "strong." It takes a great deal of energy to stuff tears down and keep those emotions deep inside. Yet it is tempting to do just that, because it hurts. It takes true strength to grieve and mourn, to acknowledge the vulnerability, allow the pain, and face the void that can never be filled in the same way again. It takes true determination to accommodate to the loss, assimilate it into life, and learn to live without what can no longer be. In other words, it's not the strong person who doesn't cry; it's the strong person who does.

Besides, tears are nature's stress-relief mechanism, containing physiological chemicals that relieve stress. That's why we call it "having a good cry." (Interestingly, the tears that stream down your face when you slice an onion have none of the stress-relieving chemicals; these only occur in tears of emotion.)

Finally, grief that is repressed, denied, or ignored does not go away. It stays buried within, and eventually it finds a means of expression. We may experience physical symptoms such as headaches, neck aches, backaches, and stomachaches. We may experience outbursts of anger, impatience with someone who doesn't deserve it, or even clinical depression. It may cause out-of-proportion reactions to something else that happens. Sadly, repressed grief may result in a life never fully lived again because of the fear of loss and hurt.

As noted in the discussion on grieving styles, some men and women cry a great deal, while others cry very little. Yet everyone benefits from having a safe and confidential relationship with someone who encourages their grieving process and gives them permission to cry when they need it.

One caution: Our most instinctual response when someone cries is to hand that person a box of tissues. However, there are two problems inherent in that.

First, they are compelled to take the tissues to be polite, regardless of whether they want them. In other words, you take your friend out of control.

Second, and more importantly, offering the tissue box gives an unintended message: "Stop it. Dry your tears. Use this. You are making me uncomfortable." Not every person will hear it that way, but too many do. In fact, in support groups grieving people sometimes refer to the box of tissues as the "shut-up box!"

So how do you put all of this information together to help those you care about?

If they are coming to your home, have a box of tissues handy and within reach. If you are meeting them elsewhere, have tissues in your pocket or purse. As you sit down, pull them out and say, "I thought I'd bring these just in case one or both of us need them." When tears well up, either say, "You can use my tissues if you want; it's up to you." Or "I don't know about you, but I need a tissue. Would you like one too, or not?" The principle is to always make tissues accessible, but never force them.

You can also expand or follow up by saying some or all of the following: "People think they need to apologize for their tears. They think they're being 'strong' when they refuse to cry. They're wrong. You show such strength and courage when you face the pain and those difficult emotions. Grief is hard work and it takes real toughness to deal with it. It's not the strong ones who don't cry, you know; it's the strong ones who do. And did you know that tears are nature's stress-relief mechanism? There are actually stress-relieving chemicals in tears, and we all need less stress! Besides, your biggest goal in life right now is to get through this, to find a way to put the pieces back together, to heal and find joy again, and I want to support that. So when we're together, you don't need to waste energy stuffing down whatever emotions come up. With me, you can cry any time. No apology necessary."

Of course, if you are grieving the person's death, too, and you would like to cry, please do! It models for your friend that tears are OK. It lets them know their loved one's life touched someone else and left a void in another heart. It shows they are not alone in their grief, and they find comfort in sharing the tears.

A final note: Some comforters fear that giving people permission to cry will result in a nonstop flow of tears. Actually, it has never happened in the history of the world that anyone started crying and was unable to stop! In fact, when grievers have permission to cry, they may need to cry less. When they do cry, they relieve stress and are better able to focus and concentrate. Most important, when you offer a safe and confidential container for their pain, your friends and family members learn you are a trusted resource who understands them in ways most other people don't.

Helpful Strategies

There are a number of strategies you can suggest that your loved ones implement to cope with their grief. Not everyone is helped by the same things, but many grievers find at least some of these useful.

1. Write in a journal.

Consider giving your grieving friends or family members a nice journal with a good pen, even if they've never kept one before or they don't consider themselves "good writers." Here are three reasons why a journal is a good idea.

a. Paper is unconditionally accepting and it is accessible 24/7. When people need to process something or when others are not available to talk, they can write. No one ever has to see it, so they can pour out their emotions, experience, anger, or whatever they wish, and it can be very cathartic.

b. It can be a good sleep aid. Grieving people generally experience one of two sleep problems. Either they go to bed but can't get to sleep, or they are so exhausted that they fall asleep immediately but wake up in the middle of the night and may be restless for hours. In either case, they most commonly notice a flood of thoughts running through their minds that they can't shut down. In addition, they may be worried about remembering to do something.

Writing for a bit before bed helps get those thoughts out on paper, and it may calm the mind down enough to sleep. If they wake up in the middle of the night, they can write again, hopefully with the same calming result.

c. It can be a good aid for finishing unfinished business. There are usually things survivors wish they had said or done before their loved one died. This is especially true if it was a sudden death. Writing can help. Some examples:

- Survivors who feel cheated out of the chance to say goodbye can write a letter to the loved one, saying everything they wish they could have said in person.

- Survivors who are angry or feel betrayed by the deceased can write in general about their anger or they may write to the deceased person specifically, with the aim to vent, explain, or express their emotions.

- Those who wish to ask for forgiveness or offer forgiveness to the deceased person can accomplish that in writing.

In any of these examples, the grieving person can decide to keep all the writings intact in the journal. Sometimes, they may feel it is more fitting to tear the pages out. They may wish, for instance, to bury a letter at the gravesite. They may burn pages to ash and bury them in a garden. A written text can be kept in a memory box with other mementoes. Something written in anger can be torn into shreds, burned, or scribbled over. Each person can implement whatever actions bring them the greatest healing and comfort.

2. Use other non-destructive ways to relieve the stress.

When people grieve, they often store stress and tension in their muscles and joints. Physical exercise is an effective reliever. It can be as simple as stomping your feet as hard and fast as you can for ten seconds, or as complex as playing a team sport. Encourage your friends and family members to adopt a regular schedule of whatever form of exercise they enjoy. It will help them relax, stay healthier, find moments of respite, and sleep more restfully.

Instead of or in addition to exercise, some people find comfort in the arts. As with writing, it doesn't have to be "good." In fact, no one ever has to see it. Some may wish to paint what the experience is like. Others may want to work with clay (or even play dough) to make something and smash it, or perhaps make something and fire it so they can keep it.

Music is a highly expressive medium. Some people listen to sad music when they want to cry, or happy music when they want to lift their spirits. Some find it cathartic to play an instrument or sing themselves. Listening to a song that was special to the deceased person can bring a flood of tears but it can also be healing, and eventually the song may bring smiles instead.

There are a wealth of options for expressing and processing the loss and grief. Encourage friends and family members to find things that work for them, and incorporate those activities into daily life.

3. Practice good comfort care (but be wary of too much "comfort.)"

Expressing and processing grief is important, but so is occasionally escaping. What brings your friends and family members comfort? It may be a soak in a hot tub with scented salts, a walk in the fresh air, or quiet time in the dark with lighted candles. It may be a particular food, a glass of wine, or watching a good comedy. Perhaps it is going to the gym or the pool.

These things are all healthy, as long as they are done in moderation. (A glass of wine is a good thing; a bottle not so much. Time to cocoon is helpful; retreating from life is not.) In addition, there must be recognition that these things do not fill the void or make it go away. They provide a brief respite from facing the pain, and often provide the needed boost of energy or strength that allows us to handle life with more equanimity.

So encourage "comfort foods" or comforting activities, while also encouraging your friends to use them wisely. They are coping aids, not grief solutions.

4. Connect to others who grieve.

Most grieving people in our death-denying society feel alone in their pain, and like no one else ever felt a similar way. It is comforting to know this assumption isn't true. Countless people have had similar experiences and have survived, thrived, and come out better on the other side. It helps to learn from their collective wisdom and gain hope from their examples.

Since everyone grieves differently, this connection could take many forms. For instance:

- Find out where and when nearby support groups meet. There are likely some "closed" groups, which require registration and a commitment to attend for a series of meetings. There may also be "open" groups that meet on a regular schedule and invite anyone to come at any time. Both types can be informative and healing, so ask at the hospitals, hospices, and churches in the area, and also keep an eye on notices in the newspaper.

- In addition to physical support groups, there is an entire array of online groups for different types of loss that provide availability around the clock. Many offer useful resources and education. If the site hosts a chat room, make sure to carefully investigate privacy policies; it can be dangerous to reveal too much about personal issues online without knowing who can access that information. Also, see whether there is a moderator or facilitator who is knowledgeable about grief so myths or stereotypes about grief don't get promoted. With reasonable caution, online support can be invaluable.

- Reading about the experiences of others can be a tremendous aid. Discover books to give or recommend to friends by checking the chapter of recommendations in this book, asking others who have been through a grief experience, finding out what books grief organizations list on their websites, or even checking online book sellers that list reviews (taking care to ensure that all the reviews were not written only by friends and family of the author). Remember that early in the grief process, concentration is compromised so smaller, easily digestible books are best. Later, more information might be desirable and a longer or more detailed book can fill the need.

Regardless of how survivors connect to each other, it is reassuring to know they are not alone and others can help light the path forward.

Addressing Fears

Grieving people often harbor fears. Newly widowed people, for instance, may fear for their safety since they are now living alone. Divorced people may have concerns about their finances, or the effects of the divorce on the children. Many grieving people feel vulnerable and fear that others will take advantage of them. In some cases the fears may be rational; in other cases, the fears are irrational.

Many would-be comforters attempt to soothe fears with logic, trying to "prove" why grievers should not feel afraid. Unfortunately, it doesn't work. You can't "logic" people out of their fears. If you doubt that, show a high-resolution picture of a snake to someone who is terrified of snakes. Logic dictates that the picture is no threat, but the person is powerless to squelch the visceral, terrified reaction. So instead of using logic, effectively address fears by acknowledging them and taking them seriously.

First, invite recognition: "Everyone in your situation has fears. Let's put them out on the table. What worries you most? What is the worst thing that could happen to you right now? What makes your stomach tie up in knots?"

Listen carefully, clarifying to make sure you understand each fear: "What I hear you saying is this . . . . Is that accurate, or how is it different?" As you ask questions and listen, help them prioritize their top two or three worries.

Recent research studies show that naming, writing down, and writing about fears objectifies them and takes away some of their emotional power. It helps move fears from the emotional center of the brain (the amygdala) to the more deliberative area (the prefrontal cortex), which helps people think more clearly and feel less threatened. Therefore, your next step is to encourage your grieving friends or family members to write down their top fears. If you gave them a journal, they may wish to write fears on a page within.

Then say, "Since these are the things that really worry you, let's look at what can we do together or with the help of others to keep you safe. What do you need to feel safe, or at least less worried?"

Brainstorm ideas together. Perhaps the widowed person needs a house alarm system, or a device for contacting someone if there is a problem. Perhaps a single-again parent needs referrals to child psychologists or family counselors, or they may need help from a financial advisor or lawyer. Perhaps those who feel vulnerable need to have a companion accompany them to appointments or they need the names of service professionals they can trust. The list could go on.

You can begin by suggesting possible solutions. Usually once you get started, your friends will join in and offer ideas of their own. Keep working on it until you get a list of the top "safety" strategies. Then have them write those strategies down on the same page as the fears. Perhaps, for instance, the fears can be on the left side and the strategies on the right. Then prioritize and devise a plan for how to accomplish the safety strategies on a schedule.

Conclude by saying, "Look at all the thing we can do to keep you safe. So every time those fears rear their ugly heads, day or night, take out this list. Look at your fears, look at what we're doing to handle those fears, and know that you're going to be OK."

Note that you may need to do this exercise over again at various points in the grief process. Once one worry is handled, it won't be long before another arises. Be a trusted support person, no matter the fears.

Putting Off Major Decisions

It is generally accepted wisdom that grieving people should put off major decisions, especially irrevocable ones.

This is sage advice. First, the "fog of grief" is a very real phenomenon based in the brain's physiological response to the shock and emotion of the loss. It results in noticeable lack of concentration and an inability to clearly evaluate decisions and their implications. Countless grieving people make decisions they later regret. Combined with the exhaustion of grief, it also means grievers are less able to withstand pressure from others, particularly family members, who insist that they make decisions before they are ready or who wish to take advantage of the situation for their own benefit.

Second, every break in attachment triggers more grief. If people make major or life-changing decisions (such as selling their homes), they invite additional pain at a time when they are already hurting. Sometimes, of course, there isn't enough money to keep the house or other considerations necessitate additional major changes. If that is the case, be prepared for the added grief it brings.

In general, though, try to follow this protocol. Help your grieving friends make a list of any time-restricted things that have to happen and when (such as filing a death claim with the insurance company, changing beneficiaries in a will, re-titling the car and house, registering kids for the new school, arranging a series of doctor's appointments, or whatever the case may be). Help make a concrete plan for when those things will happen.

Follow up with this: "Other than these things that must be done, psychologists tell us it's a wise idea to put off making major decisions for a while, especially when they are irrevocable. I agree. When anyone is grieving, concentration and rational thinking aren't as keen as they need to be to make major decisions. Besides, do you need any more grief in your life? Whenever you make major changes, you pile more grief on your plate. You have a right to wait a while. Don't let anyone pressure or push you into making big decisions. You won't regret waiting; you might regret acting too soon. It's enough to deal with your grief right now. Keep taking one step at a time, and wait until you are fully ready before making any big changes or decisions."

Don't Go Away

Remember that grief is not over in a day, a week, or a month. It takes a very long time, especially for significant deaths or losses.

The primary task of the initial twelve months is accepting, letting go, and assimilating the loss into everyday life. Part of that process involves facing all the "firsts." The first time the school band marches without their child. The first birthday. The first time attending a party. The first wedding anniversary. The first holiday season. The first Valentine's Day. The list goes on and on, and each one of those days is intensely painful.

Yet what do most people do on those days? They ignore the grieving family. They don't know what to say, so they say nothing at all. They make excuses like, "I'm sure they want to be alone on a day like today." Or "I don't want to remind them what day it is or make them cry, so I'll just stay away." Instead of feeling supported, the family feels isolated and alone in their grief.

Reach out on those days. You can call: "Hi, I know it's Jim's birthday today and I'm thinking about you. So what are your plans for the day? Are you going to the cemetery, getting together with other people, just cocooning at home, or what? What's it like for you today?" As an alternative, you can call and offer a story about Jim that makes you smile as you remember him, and ask what memories come to mind for your grieving friend.

You can send a card: "You're probably finding that a lot of people avoid you on Jim's birthday. If they do see you, they talk about anyone and everyone except Jim. I hope that you can use the enclosed gift card to grab a friend, go have coffee, and tell stories about Jim all morning. Jim is worth remembering.

I'm remembering with you, especially today." You can get many other ideas for card texts in the chapter on cards in this book.

Make sure you are there for your grieving family and friends at all those important times throughout the first year. Then don't stop there, because the grief doesn't. Don't be like so many others who assume that by the first anniversary (or sooner), they are "over it" and don't need you. It's not true. Many grieving people, especially if a spouse or child died, report that the second year can be harder than the first. They can no longer say, "A year ago, we were on vacation together," or "A year ago he gave me a rose on Valentine's Day." The reality of the death truly strikes home, and it marks a more final "letting go" as the second year begins.

The primary task in the second year and beyond, then, is to build something that wasn't there before, to set new goals that don't involve the deceased loved one, to re-craft one's identity, to finally stop asking "Why?" and concentrate on "What now?" Granted, this is a process that began in the first year, but it takes center stage in the second year, and it can be equally demanding and painful.

Companion your grieving friends and family members for the long term. Continue to say the name, remember, ask questions, listen well, and support them in whatever ways you can.

Checking in on Your Level of Support

On occasion, you'll encounter people who prefer not to be reminded of their loss or to hear the beloved's name. They may be in denial. They may be unable to process the grief and are trying to push it down. They may have developed a pattern of reacting to grief by "forgetting" and starting new. They may prefer to grieve strictly in private rather than discussing it with anyone else. In short, there are a variety of reasons why a particular person may wish you to stop being so "supportive."

You can easily check in to make sure. For instance, you can say, "I've been sending you cards, mentioning Mike's name, and acknowledging the depth of your loss. Many people find those steps to be supportive, but not everyone does. My goal is to help you the best I can, so I'd like to check in on this. Of the things I've been doing, what do you hope I keep doing because you find it helpful or comforting, and what do you wish I would stop doing now?"

Alternatively: "What do you wish I knew about what you need from me? If you could get into my brain, what would you tell me to stop doing, and what would you tell me to keep doing?" Listen well, and adjust your practices to that person's desires.

Emotional Differences between Divorce and Widowhood

Some issues facing divorced people are similar to those facing the widowed:

- Their entire social network has changed, and former friends (especially coupled friends) often drop away.

- Few others understand their grief or know how to support them, so a lot of formerly comfortable conversations become awkward.

- The impact on finances can be life-altering.

- They may need to move out of their home, which is another major loss.

- They no longer have a partner with whom to discuss issues, solve problems, or get feedback on decisions.

- They need to learn how to take over jobs or tasks that the other person always did.

- They need to build new identities as single people, including deciding which last name to use and checking off a different "marital status" box on forms.

- They have to answer awkward questions about what happened.

- Divorced and widowed parents deal with their children's grief as well as their own, usually wondering how to guide them or handle their unique needs.

- They have to let go of what can no longer be, release their sometimes carefully-planned future, and build a new and different vision for going forward.

Despite all the similarities, there are differences. For example, one common loss during divorce is intrapsychic: the shattered dreams of the happy marriage and family that they envisioned as they walked down the aisle. Questions about self-image and lovability often exacerbate the pain, especially if the divorce was initiated by the other party.

The level of anger also tends to be higher with divorce than with widowhood. Dying is seen as less of a conscious choice, so in contrast to divorce, most of the time a widowed spouse doesn't blame the other person or feel betrayed. Anger can be especially prominent in situations where one spouse surprises the other with a divorce decree or the breakup involves contentious factors, such as an affair, substance abuse, or fights over custody.

Finally, divorced people have to deal with a still-living ex-spouse, so they can't close the door on that chapter of their lives. At least for a while, every communication can be a painful reminder that reopens wounds or causes new ones. Eventually the spouses may find ways to co-parent well together or may build a friendship that wasn't possible when they were married. In other cases, friendly communication ceases to exist.

When your friends are getting divorced, maintain a degree of neutrality to the greatest extent possible. Listen well to your friend's anger and sense of betrayal, but be objectively supportive so you don't inadvertently fuel fires or get entwined in the middle. For instance, instead of saying, "What a jerk! I can't believe he did that to you!" it is better to say, "I can see how deeply you are hurt by what he did. Tell me more."

Each may want you to take sides against the other. Resist. Do not report to one spouse what the other one said. Do not offer to mediate or allow yourself to be drawn into that role. In every case, work to maintain the level of relationship that you choose to have with each spouse independently, whether that is to remain friendly with both (even if you will always naturally be closer to one than the other) or to reject ongoing friendship with one.

Overall, remember that problems in relationships are rarely unilateral, you will never know the full backstory, and taking sides isn't helpful. Your job is not to serve as judge and jury; it is to companion your friends through an extremely stressful and emotional time in their lives.

Interestingly, research shows that when an ex-spouse dies, even if it occurs long after the divorce is final, the grief of the survivor can be profound. A complex level of attachment remains, even in the most contested divorce cases. Additionally, the children of that union experience a parent's death, and the surviving ex-spouse needs to face all the implications and complications that a loss of this magnitude entails for the kids.

Neither divorce nor widowhood is "easier." They're both incredibly difficult. Regardless of which one your friends or family members face, use the principles of grief support. Keep asking open-ended questions, helping them face fears, and companioning them through whatever their situation brings.

Questions to Ask
for Positive Transitions

Even positive transitions trigger grief. Although people are excited and happy about moving to another chapter or experience, they also have to leave something behind. Be the wise friend who recognizes both sides of the emotional equation.

The following are examples of questions to ask during some of life's most common positive transitions:

A New Job or Promotion

- Starting a new job is exciting, but I imagine it is a challenge, too. You have new responsibilities, higher expectations, and different colleagues. What things are fun and interesting about your new position and what do you miss about your old one?

- This job has caused big changes in your life. What do you see as the major differences, positive and negative, both personally and professionally?

Retirement

- It's wonderful to finally reach retirement, but you have to leave a lot behind as well. What do you miss about your work life?

- You've almost achieved your goal: you will soon retire! That is thrilling, and yet closing a major chapter in your life often triggers sadness or regrets. What is the anticipation of retirement like for you? Are you thinking about what you will leave behind, even as this new, exciting chapter awaits?

- Many people approach retirement with mixed emotions, but they may be reluctant to acknowledge it to those who are envious or who tell them how lucky they are. What do you wish people knew about what it's like for you at this point?

- Sometimes people are happy to let go of the stress of their jobs, but they miss the regular interaction with their colleagues. Is it like that for you, or how is it different in your case?

- If you could give advice to someone approaching retirement, what would you tell them?

Marriage

- It is a wonderful thing to marry the person you love but there are also advantages to being single. Recognizing the normal element of grief does not mean you don't love your spouse or that you regret getting married. In fact, it helps you deal with your marriage better if you honestly recognize what you no longer have. So as you move into this new and fulfilling chapter of your life, what things are you sorry to leave behind?

  After listening, ask: I think I know at least some of the answer based on what you've told me before, but what is it about your fiancé that makes it worth it for you to leave those things behind? What are you looking forward to?

- *After several months of marriage:* We've talked before about the mixed emotions of any transition, including marriage. Now that you've been married for a while, what is it like for the two of you? In what ways are you changing as you leave behind the single life and work out your future together?

The Birth of a Baby

- I know you've been looking forward to having a family for a long time. Parenting is not easy, though. Taking a guess, I imagine you miss things like a good night's sleep or the ability to go out without planning ahead for a babysitter. Is that right, or what have you found challenging about having a baby?

- What has surprised you most about having a baby or being a parent?

- If you were writing a piece of advice for couples who are pregnant right now, what would you tell them about the experiences you've had since your baby's birth?

- Having a child changes family dynamics, including relationships with extended family. What changes have you noticed in your immediate family or extended family?

A Move from One City to Another

- It's normal to have mixed emotions about such a significant move. You are moving to something good, yet you have to say goodbye to your friendship circle, your favorite coffee shop and restaurants, and your sure knowledge of how to get around. What things, routines, or people will you miss the most? What are you most eagerly anticipating about the new place?

- Transitions like this are huge, because they affect every single aspect of your life. Expect that it will take a while before you feel the new place is "home," you feel you belong, you know your way around, and you are relaxed and comfortable. It doesn't mean it was a bad move. It just means you need to have patience with yourself and the process. You'll get there, and I'll be in touch as you build your new life.

- Some people find it useful to honor their memories when they move away from a place they have cherished. Have you thought of any ways that you can tangibly take memories with you? For instance, you could take pictures of yourself in all the locations that have been special to you and fashion them into a memory booklet. Before you leave, perhaps you could set up a trip to come back in a month or two so you can visit your old friends and eat in your favorite restaurant. Maybe you'd like to take pictures of each room in your home, take little snips of the carpet fabric, or take some of the window treatments with you. Does something like that make sense, or what other ideas appeal to you?

Empty Nest

- *Several months ahead of time:* This is such an exciting time as Matthew prepares to go off to college. Yet it means you will be a parent in an entirely different way, and it will never be the same again. What is that like for you as you anticipate the date?

- *After the child has moved out:* What was it like the first time you looked at Matthew's bedroom with the open door and the undisturbed bed? What are you finding that you miss about having his constant presence? What other things are a relief for you?

Use these suggestions as a guide, modifying them for various situations and relationships. Be there for your friends and family in all transitions, both positive and negative, with uncommon understanding and skill.

Special Issues

Those Needing Professional Help

Even though they are not clinically depressed or affected by a diagnosable condition, sometimes your friends may benefit from independent guidance as they go through grief. In fact, it is often incredibly helpful for people in transition to talk with an objective, knowledgeable person who does not have the baggage that family members may carry, and who can help them get through with greater grace and ease. However, they may not have the energy or concentration necessary to seek out such resources. You can provide great assistance by doing the legwork for them, and compiling a list of options in your area for support groups, grief coaches, and counselors.

Here's how to find them:

- Call area hospitals and hospices, which often provide a variety of bereavement support services for death, divorce, family counseling, children's grief, etc.

- Call area churches, which provide support groups themselves and/or have lists of resources to which they refer their members

- Call colleges that award counseling degrees and ask for the names of top graduates in the field of grief counseling

- Ask others you know who have experienced a trauma or loss for the names of people or groups that were helpful to them

- Watch the newspaper for notices of support group meetings in your area

Don't wait until you think someone is "stuck" or deeply struggling before you give them that list. They will be more receptive if you offer it right away. When you do, introduce it with these or similar words: "Grief and transition are hard on everyone, and healing takes a long time. It can be invaluable to talk with an objective and knowledgeable person who isn't going to judge you and who usually has helpful strategies to try. In fact, it seems to me that people who make use of resources like counselors and support groups get through the experience easier and faster than those who don't. Who knows? Even if this list isn't useful for you, someone in your family might appreciate it. So here you go. For what it's worth, this is a list of resources I've found in case it might help you or someone else."

On occasion, you will encounter people who need more help than a support group or grief coach can offer. For instance, they may sink into clinical depression, which requires psychiatric intervention and potentially anti-depressant medications. While every grieving person experiences deep sadness, trouble sleeping, lack of energy, and decreased enjoyment, diagnosable clinical depression is persistent, occurs continuously for at least two weeks, and interferes with the person's ability to function normally. Here are some signs to watch for:

- Being unable to get out of bed in the morning (No one who is grieving really wants to get out of bed, but some people truly cannot.)

- Neglecting personal hygiene and appearance

- Gaining or losing weight rapidly

- Significant change in personality

- Losing interest in everything and everyone

- Talking about suicide (Many bereaved spouses or parents say they wish they were the ones who had died instead or they wish they had died along with their beloved. This is normal. If the person has a plan for how they'd do it, or they seriously are contemplating suicide, they need professional help.)

If you notice the above signs, talk to your friend about seeing a psychiatrist to help him or her get back on track. It may also be appropriate to contact other family members to express your observations and concerns so you can work together to get the appropriate treatment in place.

Luckily, extreme cases are rare. Still, it's good to be aware of signs indicating that normal grief is crossing into the realm of clinical depression or complicated mourning, which require outside help.

When the Loss Involves Young Children

In the past, conventional wisdom said that kids are resilient and if you leave them to their own devices, they'll be fine. It isn't true. Even young children mourn for what or whom they lost, and they need information, support, and attention.

When adults try to "be strong" for their kids by holding back their own tears and emotions, kids get false messages. It creates a scenario where children who feel confused, hurt, and sad observe the adults around them acting as if nothing happened. They begin to fear that something is wrong with them. They may wonder whether other family members truly loved the person who died or whether they were just pretending while the person was alive. They may wonder whether they themselves are loved and whether anyone would miss or mourn for them if they died. They may decide that to be "grown up," they need to repress their feelings and deny their grief.

With all these confusing and conflicting messages, children can feel isolated and alone. They worry about the tsunami of emotions that they experience but dare not express. They have abundant questions that go unanswered.

Loving adults need to attend carefully to grieving children. If grownups answer questions at a child's level and help children learn at a young age how to grieve in healthy ways, those children will grow into more competent adults.

Maria Nagy, a major researcher on children's grief, gives the following brief description of death concepts by age:

Under 5 years old

Children under five have a limited ability to understand death. They perceive the dead person as living somewhere else. They do not conceive of death as definitive but as something that can be reversed. Separation is painful, and they want to go visit the person wherever he or she lives now. They ask repeated questions about where the deceased person is or when they can talk to the person again. They commonly report seeing the dead person or talking with him or her.

They need reassurance that their experience is valid, honest and simple information, and answers to their questions as often as they ask.

Five to nine years old

Children at this age realize they cannot go visit a dead person, and they gradually come to understand that death is irreversible. However, they don't perceive death as inevitable for everyone. Death is outside or separate from them—a "thing" that can "get you." They may become afraid of images like the Boogie Man or Grim Reaper. Some exhibit exaggerated fear of the dark, or they may regress to an earlier stage of development (such as in wetting the bed or sucking their thumb). They may get angry with someone who died because the person failed to escape fast enough, allowing Death to catch him or her. They often engage in games that allow expression of their confusion and emotions. In fact, you can learn much about children's perceptions by observing their play or playing with them. As with their younger companions, children at this age need reassurance and information. They also need security and love instead of punishment for their grief symptoms.

At the same time, they love to talk about the person who died. Share their stories, fill them in with additional information, and encourage their memories of the one who died. Don't be reluctant to also share the grief. Cry with them. Tell them you miss him or her, too. Offer that either of you can ask the other for a hug whenever it would feel good. Remind them that it's normal for one person to sometimes feel happier when another person is feeling sadder, and that grief is an unpredictable but healthy experience that happens because we loved someone.

More than nine years old

Abstract thinking progresses enough by this age that children can perceive death as universal, irreversible, and realistic. Separation is intensely painful because they know it cannot be alleviated. They may try to act "grown up." Yet despite their best outward attempt to mimic the "strong" (and therefore misguided) behavior of adults, their feelings inside are raw, persistent, and especially confusing. They may be angry if they believe the person who died did something avoidable that contributed to or caused the death. They may have many questions about the facts of the death, and their questions need honest answers or they will invent scenarios that are worse than the truth. It is often helpful for them to talk to someone they trust—often someone other than a parent.

It is also helpful to create a way to carry enduring memories, such as a "memory box" of mementoes, pictures, and letters they write to the deceased. Affirm for them that healing does not mean forgetting; instead they carry the meaning and memory of that person with them for the rest of their lives. Overall, then, they need permission and support to mourn, express their feelings, and learn how to go on without the physical presence of the one they loved.

Additional tips for teens

Teens are figuring out how to become independent adults with an identity of their own. They may therefore turn more frequently to peers for support and comfort, or rely on adults outside the family who are willing to listen. Regardless, they may feel more comfortable communicating about their grief in ways that are not face-to-face, such as texting, email, written notes, or short videos. Teens crave privacy, and may prefer solo activities like journaling or music. They may be particularly moody and forgetful, and may need reminders to care for themselves by staying hydrated, getting sufficient sleep, eating well, and exercising. Be patient, loving, honest, and supportive. Yet be aware that some teens develop challenges such as anxiety or clinical depression, troubles at school, suicidal thoughts, addictions, or risky behaviors. If you notice problematic signs, use the services of a qualified mental health professional who specializes in adolescent grief.

Finally, research shows that teens do better after a death when the adults in their lives share their grief, model healthy ways to cope, and provide reassurance that they are not alone. Try to be that adult for a teen you love.

Overall, the best way to help kids deal with death and grief is to prepare them well ahead of time, as they grow. Even young children can observe dead animals, leaves falling from trees, and the cycle of life. It's best for parents to encourage or proactively raise questions about what death is and what happens to a dead body, and then answer with the truth in simple terms the child can understand, perhaps involving stories from nature.

If a pet dies, it is counter-productive to promote immediate replacement. Instead, use it as a learning opportunity. Let them design their own "funeral" for the animal, complete with stories that celebrate its life and recognition of how life will now be different. Allow time for grief and tears, crying with the child if you miss the pet, too. Don't rush the process, but follow the child's lead for when they feel their grief has subsided enough that their heart is ready to love another pet.

Preparation is especially important before children attend services. Explain to them what they will see and hear. Tell them some people may be crying and others may laugh, but everyone will be remembering the person who died in their own way. Tell them they can stay for a while, or they can leave if they want. If a body is present, give them permission to touch it but let them know the body will feel like a plastic doll, not like a living body, because now that body is dead. It is important that they know that death means a person's body doesn't function anymore. They can no longer eat, go to the bathroom, breathe, sleep, hug, run, or do anything that our bodies normally do.

Ideally, young children are taken to services for people they don't know well, so they can get all their questions answered in an emotionally neutral environment. Then, when someone they love dies, they don't need to ask big questions about death, bodies, and caskets because they already know the answers. Instead, adults can concentrate on the child's emotional needs.

One very helpful strategy: When a child asks a question, respond with a question of your own. Ask, "What do you think?" For instance, when a child asks, "How did Grandma die?" Answer, "What do you think?" Or "What have you heard?" This strategy gives insight into what the child is truly asking, and alerts you to misconceptions they may have. Your answer can then be more pointed and effective, addressing the underlying issues that prompted the question in the first place.

A caution against euphemisms: children are concrete thinkers. If someone tells children that a loved one went to sleep, they will not sleep peacefully. If they are told someone expired, they will wonder about their own "expiration date." If they hear that someone was called home, they will fear answering the phone. Adults need to use real words and honest explanations, starting with a brief answer and progressing to more detail as the children ask more questions. Death should be an open topic, while always following the child's lead.

Children rarely grieve constantly, tending to alternate bursts of grief with playtime. They need permission and even built-in play breaks so they can forget for a while. Actually, that's not a bad strategy for adults as well. It's helpful for everyone to have times of respite and relaxation in the midst of grief.

Just as you researched resources on grief for your adult friends, you may wish to gather information on the child grief services that are available in your area. You can check with many of the same organizations and facilities—hospice organizations and hospitals offer support groups for grieving children of various ages, and plentiful grief counselors specialize in children.

Consider giving your friends books and resources that may help their kids, especially resources with journaling and child-centered grief activities. You can check the bibliography in this book for resource ideas. You can also use or recommend websites such as:

- http://www.hospicenet.org
- http://www.dougy.org
- http://www.griefnet.org, and
- http://www.compassionbooks.com.

Death by Suicide

A few sobering statistics:

- Suicide is currently the second leading cause of death in the United States for people aged fifteen to twenty-nine.
- In November 2016, suicide became the #1 cause of death in the United States for young people aged ten to fourteen.
- Someone in the United States dies by suicide every seventeen minutes.
- Although elderly people die of too many chronic or terminal illnesses for suicide to be a leading cause of death, the suicide rate per capita is higher for those over age eighty-five (especially widowed white men) than any other age group.

- The suicide rate in soldiers and ex-soldiers is alarmingly high and continues to grow.

- Only a quarter of suicide victims leave a note, so the majority of survivors never know why their loved ones took their own lives.

- Grief over a suicide is longer and more complex due to the stigma and emotional complications involved. In fact, studies show it can take three to five years for a parent's acute grief to subside after a child dies by suicide.

A note about terminology: Psychologists increasingly caution against saying "committed suicide." We commit murder, larceny, or other crimes. While suicide may be "a crime" in the figurative sense, in literal terms it is a tragedy with complex implications. So instead of saying "committed suicide," use the term "died by suicide" or "took his or her own life."

Other information about suicide: Research shows that people who die by suicide do not want to be dead. They want to be out of pain and see no other way to escape. In other words, suicide happens when the pain exceeds that person's resources for dealing with the pain. They develop a very narrow tunnel vision, where all they see and all they imagine for their future is pain. If they think of loved ones at all (and they may not have capacity to consider their loved ones), they convince themselves that everyone will be better off after the suicide. They believe they are doing their loved ones a favor, freeing them to go forward with life.

In the vast majority of cases, there is a diagnosable mental problem, such as clinical depression or bipolar disorder, often combined with enough abuse of alcohol or drugs to numb the strong human instinct to live. Many times this is an intensely private struggle. A suicidal person frequently fears disappointing others, appearing vulnerable, being a burden, or being exposed, and can become expert at hiding the pain.

Therefore, although it is sometimes obvious beforehand when a person is deeply troubled, in many cases suicide catches the family completely off guard and they cannot understand why it happened. Survivors may be wracked with guilt that they didn't know more, that they missed or failed to heed signs, or they couldn't prevent it. They can be overwhelmed with anger at the person who died and the perceived insensitivity or betrayal of the act. They may be paralyzed by embarrassment and shame, or wonder what other people will assume about the family or the situation. Because of the stigma and obvious discomfort most people exhibit when the topic is raised, grieving survivors are reluctant to admit or talk about what happened.

When you talk with friends or family after a suicide, take the following steps:

- Do not be afraid to name the reality, noting the terminology suggested above. When you name it first, you let friends know they can talk honestly with you without mincing words, which is something they don't often find. For instance, ask "What do you wish people knew about what it's like for you now that Matthew took his own life?" Or "Sometimes survivors of a suicide death feel like people are judging them or they feel that even saying the word suicide makes others too uncomfortable. What is it like in your case? Are there people you can talk freely with, do you find that people avoid talking about it, or is it somewhere in between?"

- Avoid all the unhelpful phrases previously discussed. Especially avoid, "At least she's no longer in pain," because it implies that suicide is a reasonable step to take when one is hurting. Suicide is always a tragedy and always the wrong choice, even though the suicide victim couldn't see any other way out.

- Ask open-ended questions and listen well, but take care not to ask what was happening that may have made the person decide on suicide, whether there was a note, or how your friend makes sense of what happened. All of those questions induce more guilt than comfort. If your friend brings them up and needs to talk through those issues, always listen. But do not ask.

- Relate stories and memories if you knew the person who died, or ask for stories and memories from your friends or family about what they will remember of their loved one's life.

- Acknowledge the normalcy of swirling emotions like guilt, anger, shock, and grief.

- The overriding principle is to ask good questions and listen deeply to the answers. Gain more ideas on what to say by reading the texts for condolence cards following a suicide.

- As with other situations of grief, consider doing the research so you can provide a reference list of support groups and counselors in your area, which often are even more beneficial for survivors of a loved one's suicide than for survivors of another type of death. Counseling and support groups allow the family to express and deal with their guilt, anger, and musings about what else they could have done to prevent it. Remind them that it's not a sign of weakness to talk with someone who better understands their experience. In fact, it is often immeasurably helpful to have someone else light the path for them, so they can eventually emerge from the quagmire.

On occasion, you may encounter friends who speak of taking their own lives. Always take suicidal talk seriously. Ask directly whether it's just wishful thinking or whether they think they could actually do it. If they could do it, ask whether they know how they would carry it out. Bringing it up will not give them ideas of suicide if those ideas are not already present. Instead, they may tell you what they are really thinking (if they aren't hiding it). If there is a plan in mind, the risk is extremely high.

It may forestall the act if you explain to the suicidal friend that you know he or she must be in tremendous pain to consider dying to get out of it. Then tell the person that you know of some resources that may be able to lessen the pain or even eventually make it go away. Ask them to imagine a possibility that they could live without pain, and ask if they will allow you enough time to see whether you can help make that happen. Though it may seem counter-intuitive, in clinical practice psychologists often tell suicidal patients that if the counseling doesn't help they can always decide on suicide later, but if they die now they will never know if it could have worked. For seriously suicidal people, that strategy is worth a try.

Even if they don't have a plan, get help any time you're concerned. Call family members. Text a national suicide hotline by texting "help" to 741741, or call a national hotline (800-SUICIDE or 800-273-TALK) together. For LGBT friends, call the national hotline specializing in LGBT issues at 866-488-7386. No matter who you call or text, don't let your friend be wtihout a companion. Follow the hotline contact's recommendations for whether to call 9-1-1 or the police department. Do your best to follow up to help ensure they get treatment. Remember, suicide happens when a person's pain exceeds their resources for dealing with the pain. Although many suicides cannot be prevented, providing resources for dealing with the pain may help. Do the best you can. You may or may not be able to prevent a suicide death.

Several advocacy organizations offer education and support, both for prevention and for support of families after a suicide:

- American Foundation for Suicide Prevention: http://www.afsp.org

- Suicide Prevention Lifeline: http://www.suicidepreventionlifeline.org

- Suicide Prevention Services of America: http://www.spsamerica.org

- Suicide Prevention Resource Center: http:// www.sprc.org

- National Institute for Mental Health: http://www.nimh.nih.gov/ health/topics/suicide-prevention

- American Association of Suicidology: http://www.suicidology.org

- The Trevor Project for LGBT youth: http://www.TheTrevorProject.com

Murder or Violent Death

Families of murder victims often receive tremendous sympathy, even from strangers. While this may be comforting, survivors also lack privacy because so many people recognize them as the family of a murder victim. Especially in high-profile cases, they can feel their own lives are stripped away as well.

The levels of denial and shock are greater after a murder than after an accident or natural death. The concept that another person's decision can snuff out a loved one's life in an instant seems incomprehensible. Survivors are commonly tossed by waves of anger at the injustice and unfairness of their situations and at the murderer personally. They speak of their loved one as stolen or ripped from their grasp. If the murder was particularly heinous, they may have nightmares imagining their loved one's final hours or minutes.

Police investigations, pretrial hearings, and the drawn-out process of seeking a verdict complicate the grief process for murder survivors. Each hearing, especially if it involves evidence, pictures, and stories of the crime, is another blow, throwing them back into the vortex of pain.

During a judicial process that can take years, suspects may remain free, and it is immensely painful for survivors to encounter them or hear about their normal activities of life. Sometimes legal proceedings end when a perpetrator negotiates a plea bargain to a lighter sentence or the verdict is "not guilty," both of which can seem like a miscarriage of justice to the surviving family. Other times the murderer is never found. All these factors complicate the grief process.

Even a guilty verdict with a resultant prison sentence or death penalty does not provide closure to the grief because it doesn't begin to address the loss of the person who died. Murder survivors sometimes are caught in the web of trying to understand murder rather than attending to their grief. They focus so much on who the perpetrator is, why the perpetrator committed the crime, how it could have been prevented, what is required for "justice," and other issues surrounding the murder that they don't take time to acknowledge, accept, and work through their personal loss.

In almost all cases of murder, survivors cope better when they receive professional help and/or attend support groups. They need understanding, compassion, hope, and the assistance of others to avoid being trapped and suffocated in the mire.

If you have friends or family affected by murder, accompany them through the process to the greatest extent you can:

- As for other complicated cases, try to discover resources in your area.

- Offer a good book on this type of grief (see the bibliography in this reference guide for starters).

- Ask good questions and listen well.

- Send a card or give them a call on the day before or after every court date, or if possible, go along with them.

- Say the name of the person who died and share stories and memories.

- Use the word "murder."

- Be a safe, confidential, understanding person your friends can trust.

Helpful websites:

- Families after Murder: http://www.familiesaftermurder.com

- Support after Murder and Manslaughter: http://www.samm.org

- "Homicide Survivors—Dealing with Grief," a comprehensive PDF created by the Canadian Resource Centre for Victims of Crime: http://www.crcvc.ca/docs/homsurv.pdf

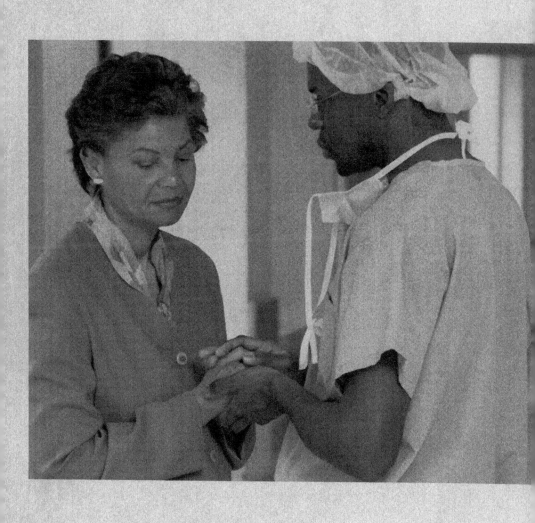

Serious or Terminal Illness

Background Information

Seventy percent of Americans die of a chronic or terminal illness, so it's likely that many of your friends will as well. They will deeply appreciate your companionship both initially and throughout this most critical time.

The family's grief process begins with the diagnosis. They vacillate between numbing shock and a raging river of emotions. It seems surreal and almost impossible to believe, especially if the diagnosis comes when the person is feeling reasonably healthy. The reality of the diagnosis sinks in as treatments begin, though it is often mitigated by hope for a cure. Deeper emotions are set off when the person's condition deteriorates or when a cancer recurs.

Most friends who hear of a diagnosis will try to cheer the ill person on, regale them with stories of others who beat the odds, and urge them to fight. In other words, too many would-be comforters end up telling their ill friends how they should react, what they should hope for, and how they should feel. They talk and urge and prompt, but they do not listen. Don't let that be you. Your task is to be honest about what is happening, find out what your friend is experiencing and what your friend hopes for, and support that.

Being honest or facing the reality of a prognosis does not mean you take away someone's hope. The truth is that hopes change over time. At first, the hope is always for a cure. When cure becomes impossible, the hope may be to live long enough to see a certain event (such as a wedding, graduation, or birth), to do something specific, or to talk with a particular person. If that is achieved or it becomes impossible, the hope may be to not die in pain, or to die with family around, or to be remembered. All along the way, find out what your friend hopes for, and support those hopes even as they change due to time and circumstances.

Your goal is also to create a safe and confidential space where your friends and their families can talk about whatever they need to discuss, including their fears and the practicalities of what could indeed happen before they wish it would. Incorporate the open-ended questions previously discussed in this book, review the list of phrases to avoid and the information on anticipatory grief, and be willing to listen in ways that others don't.

When you are unafraid to listen and to engage in these sometimes difficult conversations, you actually make it better for your ill friend. Research with terminally ill people shows that thirty to sixty minutes of discussing their personal experience measurably decreases their levels of suffering and depression. Take the time to ask good questions and really listen to the answers, and you will help them cope.

If you are close, or a member of the family, you can also serve them well by encouraging family conversations about quality of life and medical treatment wishes. Survivors of a loved one's death grieve with less regret, guilt, and second-guessing if they are not required to make treatment decisions for their loved ones without knowing what they want. Therefore, when there is a serious or terminal diagnosis, it is particularly imperative to have these discussions and get the person's wishes in writing.

Sometimes patients and their families resist talking about treatment wishes and end-of-life options because of fear or discomfort with the topic. Sometimes there is a measure of superstition that talking about death will somehow make it happen or take away the person's hope. However, having the conversations and getting wishes in writing can have an immensely positive effect for everyone. It keeps the patient in control to the greatest extent possible. It relieves the burden from everyone because they know how to help their loved ones have what they want. It banishes the big white elephant from the room and replaces it with understanding and greater intimacy. There is no downside; there is only gain.

These decisions are very individual. Some people want every intervention known to humankind to keep their bodies alive for as long as the body can be kept alive, no matter the condition or the level of their abilities. Most people, though, have some vision for when they would want to forego any artificial intervention and allow their body to die of the underlying disease(s). It might be as simple as, "Turn off the machines and stop treatments when I can no longer communicate in meaningful ways with those I love," or "When I no longer recognize my family members 50% of the time," or "When I will never again be able to eat." It could be stated in the reverse too: "Keep machines and treatments going as long as I can have a coherent conversation," or "I am able to be up and out of bed for at least a couple of hours every day," or "I can watch football and drink a beer," or "There is a better than 50-50 chance that I can be my normal self for at least a month longer," or "The pain and suffering of the treatment lasts for a shorter period of time than the number of days or weeks the treatment is likely to buy me." Everyone is different, but just about everyone knows what they want if they really think about it.

In other words, the most important question to ask is what "quality of life" means to your ill friends. Encourage them to think about it, to write it down (preferably in a formal document like a living will or a Five Wishes document), and to let both their doctors and their family know what they want. In addition, they should fill out the form to appoint a Power of Attorney for Healthcare, also known as a healthcare proxy. (This form is contained within the Five Wishes document, or a standard form may be used.) The healthcare proxy is the person with the specific responsibility to make decisions for the patient when the patient is unable to do so. As long as your friends are competent, conscious, and capable, they will be making their own decisions. It is only when they are not conscious or capable of decisions that the healthcare proxy comes into play. The proxy must therefore be highly trusted, and must know what the patient wants *and why*. Knowing why is even more important, since it is impossible to foresee ahead of time every situation that may arise. If the proxy knows why, the decisions can fall in line with what the patient wants even if the specifics of the situation are different. Encourage those conversations to happen. (And while you're at it, fill out these forms for yourself, even if you are healthy. Everyone should have these documents in place, in order to maintain control of their own care and take the burden off their family's shoulders.)

Facilitating Communication

It is difficult for people who are ill or undergoing treatments to keep everyone else apprised of their results, prognosis, overall situation, and progress without having to tell the same story fifty times, especially if they have a large network of friends, relatives, co-workers, and acquaintances. You can provide an invaluable service by helping your ill friends and/or the family to set up a Caring Bridge site. (See http://www.caringbridge.org.)

This free service provides a personal website to which friends and family members can subscribe. The ill person posts updates as frequently as desired. Whenever there's a new post, all those registered for that person's site receive an e-mail informing them that new information is available. They log onto the website, read the information posted there, and have the opportunity to respond with a message of their own. The patient or family can respond to those posts or give a general response, delete unwanted posts or hide the more private ones, and manage the messages however they wish.

This service streamlines the information process, disseminates updates immediately to everyone concerned, and facilitates dialogue and support.

Watch for Fatigue When You Visit

People with serious or terminal illness, especially those undergoing chemo-therapy, experience heightened levels of fatigue. Shorter, more frequent visits are much better than long ones. When you do visit, check in after a while by asking questions: "Mike, we've been visiting for about half an hour. What is your energy level right now, and what would you most like to do? I can leave so you can rest, I can just quietly sit here by you, I can read to you if you'd like or play some music, or we can keep talking about whatever you want to talk about. Let me know what you would like."

Giving options like this and allowing your friend to be honest with you is so much better than having to deal with those who over-stay or who don't know how to be a quiet presence. Remember, your job is not to cheer your friends up or have them feel better when you leave. Your job is to companion them wherever they are and serve their needs. It's all about them; it's not about you.

Concrete Help

When your friends are ill or dying, do not detach. Continue to send cards, make phone calls, and support them and their families. Consider taking concrete actions tailored to what you believe or know to be helpful. Here are a few ideas:

- Arrange for an afternoon of care or provide it yourself so family caregivers can get a bit of respite to do whatever they wish.

- Use web sites such as TakeThemAMeal.com, MealTrain.com, CareCalendar.org, or LotsaHelpingHands.com to coordinate care.

- Fill in as needed, perhaps delivering a prepared meal yourself on a day when others don't.

- Give a subscription to a service such as Peapod that delivers groceries to the home.

- Arrange for anything from a cake to a full-blown party if someone in the family has a birthday during the illness.

- Offer to drive your friend to appointments or treatments, and/or to drive the family's kids to their activities.

- Help write out thank-you notes for people who bring food or do something for the family.

- If your friend would like to send an email or a card to someone, allow the patient to dictate it to you. This saves energy and allows your friend to remain lying down.

- If a person is in the hospital, put together a hospital care kit. Include things like bottled water or juices, protein bars, packages of popcorn or trail mix, or anything that the family can snack on or drink without having to leave the hospital room to do it. You can also throw in a book of crossword puzzles or something that can occupy their time when the patient is napping or undergoing tests. Deliver it to the hospital room or to the family's home.

Whatever you do, stay in touch. So many others will stay away. They don't know what to say or do, they are uncomfortable facing mortality, and so they don't do anything. Sick or dying patients can feel isolated or even abandoned. Be there for your friend.

Illness at Holiday Time

Illness and dying are particularly difficult at holiday time. In our society, all is supposed to be merry and bright as families gather to celebrate treasured traditions. Too many people don't want to put a damper on the merriment by talking about the illness or visiting someone in the hospital or in hospice care.

Resolve to be especially present during the season. Visit, call, and write cards. You can get other ideas in the chapter on cards, but here is one example of a card text:

> For you, this season isn't all merry and bright as your daughter's health and future hang in the balance. So instead of wishing you happy holidays, I wish you strength to get through this. I wish you restful sleep, at least on occasion. I wish you skilled and communicative doctors and nurses. I wish you wisdom to know what to do. I am right here in your corner, and I will help in whatever way I can.

If someone is in the dying process over the holidays, you can write:

> This holiday is a bittersweet one for you, as you cherish every minute together and yet recognize it will likely be the last holiday season you have with each other. It may be all the more complicated by people who are too uncomfortable to be around you or to acknowledge the reality. Through it all, I offer an open and confidential ear, a tear-absorbing shoulder, and my heartfelt care. I hope this little package helps make your hospital time just a little easier, and I will be checking in to see how else I can help. In the meantime, I wish you strength, resilience, wisdom, faith, and love.

Regardless of the season, maintain the courage to face their reality and support them through it.

Four Things That Matter Most

In pivotal research with dying people, Dr. Ira Byock (a medical doctor and psychologist) found four things that dying people need to give and receive from the people they love. Those who are able to do so can die with greater peace and dignity, while their loved ones have fewer regrets and complications in their grief afterward. These four things bring a sense of completeness to the journey.

Actually, all of these are things we ought to be doing all along. It's just more urgent to do so when someone is seriously ill or dying.

1. "Thank you."

Life review, reflecting back on the decisions, mistakes, and joys that shaped life's trajectory, is an almost universal aspect of the dying process. Especially as people approach death, they search for reassurance that their life had meaning, made an impact, or touched someone. In the course of daily life, yelling at or complaining about family, coworkers, and friends is easier and more common than thanking or complimenting them. Dying people need to be thanked. In turn, they need to offer thanks to those who have been important to them.

Sometimes surviving family members get angry when hundreds of people come through the services and talk endlessly about how wonderful their loved one was. Yet these same people avoided the person when he or she was dying, when the person needed to know their life made a difference. Why wait until the person dies to tell the family how much you cared, how much the person helped you grow, or about all the commendable characteristics that person exhibited over the years? Tell the person during life, rather than telling family after the death.

In the course of your visits, then, make sure you tell friends how important they are in your life. Thank them for the times you've spent together and for the joy they bring. Talk about stories and memories of your relationship over the years. Gratefully accept their recognition of your value in return.

Note that I said, "How important they are in your life," not how important they *were*. Avoid talking about all of it in past tense, as if your friend is no longer important or as if you are already "signing off." You can talk about the "remember when we . . ." stories and how your friend helped pull you through a difficult time, but continue to say how meaningful it is to have this relationship right now, and for as long as it lasts. You can say how much you will miss your friend, but also say how much you want to make the most of whatever time remains.

2. "I forgive you."

We are not perfect people; we're just people. Dying patients know they have hurt others, and they have likewise been hurt. In fact, the easiest people to hurt are the ones most deeply loved. Yet they sometimes hold grudges so long they don't even remember why they got upset in the first place. Dying people usually realize that grudges and bitterness are no longer worth it.

They need to ask for forgiveness for the wrongs they have done and to give forgiveness for the wrongs done to them. They need to forgive and be forgiven.

You can't force anyone else to ask for forgiveness, but you can take the initiative to do so yourself. If you think there are ways you hurt your friend, say you're sorry and ask for forgiveness. The more specific you can be, the better. However, you can also say that because you are not perfect it's likely you've unintentionally done or said things that have hurt, or that you have forgotten things, and so you want to ask forgiveness for anything at any time that wasn't loving, caring, or supportive, and especially for anything that was hurtful.

Then follow your friend's lead. It may open up conversations about things that happened in your relationship over time. It may result in mutual forgiveness, perhaps accompanied by tears and hugs. It may prompt a gruff, "Yeah, whatever," especially from someone who is not experienced in giving or receiving forgiveness. The important thing is that your friend hears you say it.

3. "I love you."

One of the greatest regrets survivors have is the failure to say "I love you" to the person who died. Sometimes, even if a couple loved each other very much, their last interaction was an argument, so the final words they exchanged were harsh, critical, or insulting. In other cases, a survivor had such a conflicted relationship that it was too difficult to voice those words before the person died. Regardless, mourners who do not or cannot express these words in some way cope with more complicated grief and more unfinished business as a result. Both dying people and those around them need to give and receive love.

If you can actually say those words, do. If your relationship is such that the two of you have never exchanged words like that and it would be awkward to do so now, at least come as close as you can. This is similar to what you do when saying, "Thank you." Do your best to say, "I love you," whether or not your friend can respond in kind.

4. "Goodbye."

When the time comes, everyone wants permission to go. People will sometimes hang on despite pain and suffering until they feel their loved ones will be OK and are ready to let them go. Saying goodbye does not make loved ones die; they are going to die anyway. It just gives them permission to do what they need to do with peace and grace. It can be as simple as saying, "I hope you can live for a long time yet, but if it's too much for you, if you can't do it anymore, then let go. It's OK. We will miss you and we will cry, but we will be all right. Go in peace."

Sometimes very responsible people need to be released from their responsibilities. For example: "It's not your job to raise the kids anymore. We will all work together to raise them for you, and to keep your memory alive in their hearts. You can go, knowing your kids will be well cared for."

Do what you can to help this step occur for your friend and the family.

Hospice

Hospice is an interdisciplinary team operating under a doctor's supervision to provide palliative care. Hospice has dual goals: helping patients live as fully as possible until they take their last breaths, and facilitating a process where patients may die with dignity, grace, and peace. The hospice team can include nurses, social workers, psychologists, family members, and volunteers, depending on each patient's particular needs.

Palliative care treats the symptoms rather than trying to cure the underlying disease. It effectively controls pain levels, eases breathing, keeps lips and skin moist, and does everything possible to relieve the person's suffering. While anyone can receive palliative care at any point in the course of illness or treatment, hospice care utilizes palliation to try to ensure that none of their patients dies in pain.

Hospice workers also effectively accompany the dying person and the family. They answer questions, provide medications, facilitate communication, and coordinate care in order to maintain quality of life for the dying person and the family throughout the process.

Note that hospice isn't a place; it's a service. Most hospice care occurs in the dying person's home, although many hospitals, nursing homes, and independent facilities contain a hospice unit for people who can't go home or don't have others to care for them.

People must meet two criteria to qualify for insurance coverage of hospice care:

1. A prognosis from a doctor of fewer than six months to live *and*

2. A commitment to forgo treatments aimed at a cure.

In other words, people cannot enter hospice care if they are still undergoing chemotherapy or any other curative treatment.

Because of this, too many people believe hospice is where you go when you've given up. That attitude keeps people from entering hospice care until they are so close to death the organization cannot accomplish the good work it was created to do. Accepting the inevitable reality of death and making a concrete decision to live as fully as possible is a positive and strength-filled choice—quite the opposite of "giving up."

Likewise, hospice is not what people do when hope is gone. Instead, hospice workers help maintain the hopes of dying people even as those hopes change over time, and help the patient and the family make the most of all the time remaining, Obviously, this is difficult to do given only a few hours or a couple of days. It is best if people enter hospice care when they still have weeks or months left to live, so they can take advantage of all that hospice offers. In fact, in several studies, patients in hospice care lived longer than those who either didn't enter hospice or entered only at the very end of their lives.

A highly recommended resource is the book *Final Gifts: Understanding the Special Awareness, Needs, and Communications of the Dying* by Maggie Callanan and Patricia Kelley. These two hospice nurses with decades of experience educate readers on the death process and on how to better understand the unique communications of dying people. Anyone facing the death of a loved one will learn invaluable information in its pages. Read it yourself. Give a copy to the family. Give a copy to your friend. (The full reference is in the bibliography.)

When Your Pen Hovers Over the Page: Condolence Cards and When to Send Them

General Information and Schedule

Many people make it a practice to send condolence cards or create a sympathy post on social media when friends experience a death in the family. Too many don't know what to write, and they stop after the card or post they delivered in that first week. In this section, you learn how to make an ongoing difference in your friends' lives.

Depending on the person and the situation, you may wish to send something at the following times:

- Two to three days after the services

- Three to four weeks after the services

- On some of the monthly anniversaries of death

- On special days like birthdays (including the birthday of the person who died), wedding anniversaries, graduations, holidays, Valentine's Day, or any other important occasions

- On the anniversary of death for several years afterward

From this spectrum, choose the frequency and cost of contact based on the nature and value of the relationship.

Gifts you may want to include:

- Gift certificates for a dinner delivered to the home, a restaurant meal, coffee, a movie, a massage or day spa, or anything else you believe will be relaxing or comforting

- A tapestry made from the deceased person's portrait

- A small plant, especially if the family would put it into a garden

- A book on grief, preferably one closely matched to the situation (see the list in this book for suggestions)

- Notice of your donation in memory of the person who died

- A tree planted in memory of the person who died

- Teddy bears or quilts made out of the deceased person's T-shirts

- Some truly homemade foods if you like to bake or cook

- A shredding service for papers the family needs to clear out

- A single flower in a bud vase

- A monthly fruit or food basket delivery

- Whatever you believe your friends and family will enjoy

Carefully consider the bereavement card you choose, especially for the first card or two. Choose a text that is authentic and honest rather than one that denies the death or minimizes the loss. For instance, avoid texts that assert the person hasn't really died but is simply in the next room or texts that instruct mourners not to cry because their loved one is happy. Ensure that any prewritten text meets the criteria for grief support already discussed in this guide.

Later cards may have an inspirational verse or simply an attractive picture and may have few or no pre-printed words. One excellent and inexpensive source for good cards is www.CardsByAnne.com. All the cards are hand-designed and many of the sympathy cards are quite good.

Regardless of the text on the card, be sure to include personalized, hand-written comments. Let mourners know you took the time and care to write something yourself.

In the first card, you may wish to reference the services—the lovely music, the moving eulogy, or the number of people who turned out to show their support. In every card, remember to write the name of the person who died, and always keep the focus on the survivors, not on you.

The following pages contain a wealth of ideas on which to base your card texts, divided into categories for a variety of situations and timings. Use these as written, or adapt them so they sound like you and more closely fit the circumstances. These texts also contribute ideas you can add to your repertoire when talking with friends or family in your regular interactions.

Immediately After a Death

When I learned of the sudden death of your beloved [name], my heart instantly went out to you. What words could I possibly say that could comfort you at this time? There are none. So I join my tears with yours as I remember [name's] life and what [he/she] meant to so many.

When a loved one dies long before [his/her] time, it turns everything upside down. Any answers to the question "Why?" ring hollow. As you navigate this heart-wrenching time, know that every day I take a moment to let your grief remind me of what is most important in life and, in so doing, I honor the life of [name].

Though I share your sadness, I cannot enter into the depth of your grief. All I can do today is use a few minutes to honor [name's] memory by deliberately extending a kindness to another person in memory of [his/her] life. I promise that today somebody will smile because [name] lived.

[Name's] death shocked me to the core. I could not believe it. Yet if it shocked me, how much more devastated you must be! I cannot fully understand your pain, nor can I bring [name] back. What I can do is assure you of my support and offer to help you remember the wonder that was your [husband/child/other relationship]. I'll call you soon to get together for coffee.

If the number of people who attended services provided a measure of success, then [name] was more than successful. Yet, [name] didn't measure success by the number of people who loved [him/her]. Rather, [he/she] measured it by how often [he/she] could lend a hand and share [his/her] skill at [_____] with the people [he/she] served so well. Along with so many others, I join you in gratitude for [his/her] life and sadness for [his/her] death.

Does one life make a difference? [Name's] did. Though [he/she] was known and loved by many (as evidenced by the outpouring of people for the services), I think it was the depth of [his/her] commitment to the well-being of [his/her] friends that touched me most during the time I knew [name]. That is a memory I will cherish for the rest of my life.

[Name] was a gem—one of the finest [women/men] I've ever known. In fact, I will always remember the time when . . . [story]. I know that memories like this cannot erase the pain of loss, but perhaps as you allow yourself to cry and grieve, you can also allow yourself sustaining moments of laughter and joy. As you walk this journey, I will do whatever I can to make things easier for you and to honor [name's] life.

[Name] was an interesting and colorful character. Everyone knew [he/she] could be as ornery as a stubborn mule, and [he/she] certainly had issues. Yet you saw the heart beneath the outside layers. You were devoted to [him/her] and cared for [him/her], and I imagine [he/she] loved you more than [he/she] had the capacity to express. Your lives intertwined in so many ways that it is impossible for anyone else to know the depth of your loss. In the midst of this complex situation, I will do my best to help you honor [name's] life and to support you as you move into a future without [his/her] presence at your side.

[Name's] death was not a surprise, and it would be normal if you felt some relief that [he/she] is no longer suffering. Yet I know it is still intensely painful to lose your life companion of so many years. Every waking moment is different for you now, and it will take a long time to build a new sense of normalcy in your life. I will be here for you throughout this process to support you in whatever ways I can.

It is difficult to measure the "success" of a life. Yet, when I look back on [name's] life, it is impossible to see it as anything other than incredibly successful. Why? Because [name] left [his/her] little part of the world a better place. Nothing more can be asked of anyone, and [name] answered that call in [her/his] own unique way. I am better for having known [name]. I hold you in my heart as you struggle through these first months without [name] by your side.

Kahlil Gibran wrote, "When you are sorrowful, look into your heart and you shall see that you are weeping for that which has been your delight." [Name] was truly your delight. My heart is with you as you mourn [his/her] death.

I didn't know [name] well, nor did you and I have occasion to speak of [him/her] often over the years. However, in the few times that [name's] came up or when I saw you together, it was obvious that you loved, admired, and respected [him/her]. I hope the memory of your treasured relationship with [name] helps sustain you even in the sadness of grief.

Helen Keller said, "All that we love deeply becomes a part of us." [Name] has died, and there is no way to erase that reality or its implications. At the same time, you are a different person because [he/she] loved you, and no one can ever take that away from you. As long as you live, a part of [him/her] lives on in you, and in the lives of everyone [he/she] touched.

I didn't know [name] beyond our casual relationship. However, I was always impressed with how much [he/she] cared for you and the family and tried to do what was best for those [he/she] loved. As you cope with [name's] death, I will honor [his/her] commitment to your well-being by offering you a listening ear, a willing shoulder, and on occasion, a good dinner out. I'll be in touch soon.

There is no way to adequately honor the memory of [name] or the difference [he/she] made to so many, including me. Yet I want to try. So today, I am donating to [organization or foundation the person or family supported or organization that funds research on the cause of the death] in [his/her] name. In this way, many people will continue to benefit, and [name's] legacy will live on.

Even though we aren't members of the family, we have been deeply affected by [name's] death. We are donating to [the organization the family requested in lieu of flowers], and we know that as our donation joins with those of so many others, the world will be a better place because [name] lived. Our support won't stop there, though. We will continue to do everything we can in this difficult time to support you and help you move forward as [name] wanted.

This is a time of mixed emotions. It is, of course, a relief to you that [name] is not suffering anymore. It is also a relief that *you* don't have to suffer anymore watching that process. Yet you miss [him/her] and wish [he/she] were still alive. It's OK to be happy it is over and yet sad that [name] has died. Both sides of the equation are normal. Even when you feel like a ping-pong ball going back and forth between them, I hope you can honor whatever you're experiencing at each moment in time. I will do what I can to support and walk with you through this difficult and emotional process.

Tears are not a bad thing. They are an expression of love and longing. Besides, they contain chemicals that help relieve stress, they help us heal, and they give expression to the pounding ache inside. The tears will eventually stop, and peace will come. In the meantime, though, I hope you find the strength to let them spill out and join the tears of so many people who mourn [name]. We have lost a treasure, and it is fitting that our tears rain on a world that will never be the same. My sorrow joins with yours as our tears mingle together in memory.

You and [name] have been my friends for so long that my heart breaks with you over [his/her] death. I know I can't enter all what you feel and I certainly can't take away your pain. What I can do, though, is offer the strength that comes from our companionship. On this lonely journey, I hope you can feel a little less alone knowing that I walk with you.

Few people receive the gift of being loved without measure, but I know you were. In fact, the depth of your grief now is an indication of the depth of the love you shared with [name]. Though life will never be the same, may the knowledge of so great a gift help sustain you through the pain.

When my [relationship] died, it was as if I'd lost half of my body. There were days when the memories of [name] would make it better and days when they made it worse. Did I hate the pain? Yes. Yet eventually, I learned not to fear it because it was also a manifestation of the love we had. I don't know whether you feel the same way, but no matter what, I am here to help you work through the pain, minimize the fear, and remember the love.

It is said that spouses who are married for a long time start to look and act like each other. If that is the case, then you are doubly blessed because [name] was a beautiful person inside and out. [He/she] seemed to bring a sense of peace and serenity wherever [he/she] went, and I certainly experienced that during the times we met. While life is anything but serene for you right now, I wanted you to know the impact [name] had on my life. I am grateful for the gift of having known [him/her].

[Name] was an extraordinary person, one of those whom no one can ever replace. Know that my heart is with you as you happily recall your years together and yet cry through the heartache [his/her] absence brings.

Some lives are measured by how many people called them "friend." Other lives are measured by the incredible impact they had on a few. Though I only know the story of [name's] life, from what you have told me, [he/she] was a person of unassuming generosity who had a long-lasting impact on the lives of those who knew [him/her] best. That is a legacy worth celebrating with both smiles and tears. I share both with you.

When we lose a trinket, we mourn only momentarily, and then life goes on as before. When we lose a treasure, nothing is the same and the void is deep. You have lost a treasure. So have we. Together may we honor [name] as we cry, laugh, remember, and eventually heal.

It was amazing to see the number of people overflowing the services last week. It has to be gratifying to know that [name] touched so many lives and that you aren't the only one who thought [he/she] was a true gem. I hope that over the next couple of weeks you get to read the letters and cards written by those who care and know what a special gift you had, even as you realize what a loss [his/her] death brings.

[Name's] death has affected me deeply. Yet you were so much closer to [him/her] than I. You are losing a best friend, a trusted companion, an unending source of wisdom, a sounding board, a helpful mentor, and so much more. The struggle will continue for a long time to come. It is hard to let go of one so loved, yet that love will forever remain a part of us. I know we will continue to share stories and memories, and I hope I can help as you move into the future without [his/her] physical presence by your side.

Grief accompanies a long illness, and you have known its ways already as you watched [name] slowly die. The two of you gleaned deep lessons in the years-long struggle with [his/her] illness. Even as you mourn [his/her] absence, perhaps those lessons and the strength [he/she] showed then can help you move forward and live more fully now. Know that I am here to help you do that.

I never knew your [relationship] and so I cannot do what I'd most like to do— offer a happy remembrance of how [he/she] touched my life. Yet I can offer my listening ear and would love to learn more about [name]. I will call to see if you are available for [a slice of pie and coffee] sometime in the next few weeks.

Seasons continually change, chapters end and others begin, and yet life and love know no reason to die. Though [name's] physical absence leaves a gaping void, [he/she] lives on in our hearts, and we carry [him/her] forward in our lives. I am here to help you honor [name] by listening to the stories of the past, even while you build new stories for a future enriched by [his/her] memory.

Certain people come into our lives and touch us deeply. I know [name] touched so many with [his/her] amazing ability to persevere through the challenges of having a disability. What an inspiration [name] was to others with [her/her] attitude toward life! [He/she] inspired me too, and I am helping to create a living legacy by donating to [name of foundation or organization that supports people with that disability]. You've lost an incredible companion, yet the world is a better place because [he/she] lived. [Name]'s influence will live on.

Charles Dickens wrote, "And can it be that in a world so full and busy, the loss of one creature makes a void in any heart so wide and deep that nothing but the width and depth of eternity can fill it up!" The death of [name] leaves that kind of a void. As we gaze over the edge together, I offer you my love, my memories of [name], and my heartfelt care.

I have rarely heard such touching eulogies as I heard at [name's] services. I was inspired to live my own life more fully in [his/her] honor. As you move forward, I will do whatever I can to help you do the same.

At the services, I told you one of the memories of [name] that I will carry with me forever. [Reminder of the story]. Lately, I was also remembering [give another memory or story]. I'm sure that as time goes by, there will be many more stories and memories rising up. [Name] will be missed in so many ways. Through it all, I am here for you to help you live in a way that honors your memories.

It's been two weeks now since the funeral. I imagine extended family members have left, and people around you are getting back to their "normal" lives. I know your grief will last longer than a few weeks, and I will continue to be here for you as we go forward. You can always call me if you'd like, but know that I'll be calling soon to check in, listen to how you're doing, and see how I can help.

A Monthly or Yearly Anniversary of a Death

It's hard to believe that [number] months have passed since your [relative] died. Time takes on a different dimension when we lose someone we love, as if it were simultaneously a long time and yet just a moment ago when [he/she] was just a phone call or an arm's length away. Regardless of the passage of time, I will help ensure that [name's] memory and stories live on. I'm remembering with you today.

You're probably finding by now that most people are afraid to mention [name]. In fact, they will talk about anything and everything except [him/her]. They mean well. They're just afraid they will upset you or make your grief worse. They don't understand that you want and need to remember and talk about [him/her], even if tears come in the process. Despite the reluctance of so many, I hope you find opportunities to speak [his/her] name and tell the story. I'll call soon so we can share and honor [name's] life.

Do you remember at the visitation when I told you I will always remember [name's] [smile, laugh, caring heart, or other characteristic]? I shared that story with a mutual friend who heartily agreed. Nothing will ever replace [name's] [characteristic], and we will carry that memory with us forever.

On a day like today, I know there is nothing I can do to take away the pain. Still, I hope you can at least enjoy [a cup of your favorite coffee, a massage, a good meal that you don't have to cook, etc.] with the enclosed gift card. Perhaps it will even bring a smile amidst the clouds in your heart.

Your life is so dramatically different than it was [number] months ago. You have borne incredible pain, yet you have shown gritty determination. Each month that passes brings you closer to healing, closer to laughing freely, and closer to putting pieces of your life into place. It is an honor to call you my friend, and today I wanted to let you know how much I care.

It hasn't been long since [name's] death, and you've had to handle so many details and do so much paperwork. It has to seem overwhelming at times, and I will continue to help you in whatever ways I can. As each piece falls into place, you are moving into a future that will be very different than you had planned. Yet that future can still be a good one, and bit by bit you're getting there.

It was delightful to see you smile when we got together last week. I know grief and loneliness are still present, yet hope and happiness peek through on occasion. As you continue the journey, you are moving toward healing. Those sad times will become less frequent and less intense while moments of happiness and smiles become more frequent and more intense. I hope you can keep pushing forward, and I look forward to continuing to both cry and smile together.

You create a wonderful testimony to [name's] love by allowing yourself to live fully enriched by [his/her] memory. Today, I will take a moment to remember [him/her], perhaps shed a tear, and then resolve to find a way to make someone smile. There is no better honor I can offer, and I offer it with you.

Keep in mind that there will always be people who expect you to grieve in the way they believe you "should." If you don't, they may be genuinely concerned for you and/or think something's wrong with you. Be assured, though, that there is nothing wrong with you. What you're experiencing is normal for a grieving person. Follow your own path, and know that understanding people can be there with you wherever you are. I hope you'll allow me be one of them.

It's been about [number] months since [name] died. I wonder if you feel like you're on a roller coaster ride at times—some days feeling up and other days feeling down, as if you're right back where you were when you learned of [name's] death. It can make you feel like you're going crazy, but you're not. This is normal for grieving people. Whether you are "up" or "down," know that you are healing slowly but surely. Remember often, cry when you feel like it, and welcome the moments of joy that sustain you through it all.

You're probably tired of people telling you how strong you are. I imagine that sometimes you want to tell them you feel like a strand of blown glass ready to break with the slightest wind. You want to tell them that you put on your "public face" when you go out, but it's a different story when you walk back into your empty house. You want to tell them to change places with you for a while and then tell you how strong you are. They just don't understand. So let such comments slide off and clatter to the ground. Then keep putting one foot in front of the other. Every morning that you wake up and get out of bed is one more morning toward healing. Life can be good again, but it takes time. Hang in there. I'm pulling for you.

[Name] died [number] of months ago this week. Yet it's still hard to believe this powerful presence, this big smile and hearty laugh, this enveloping hug and font of wisdom, is gone from this earth. People tell us [his/her] spirit remains, but it isn't embodied in a tangible way anymore, and that's what we miss. Today, I'm remembering [him/her] with fondness and joy, and holding you tenderly in my heart.

As the reality of your [relative's] absence sinks in, as you reach for the phone to call [him/her] before you realize [he/she] isn't there to answer, there will be times of intense sadness and grief. Over time, the bad times will become less frequent and the will decrease. In the meantime, take each day as it comes, with whatever relief, sadness, joy, or memories it may hold.

The things that at first bring tears later bring smiles. I hope this [number]-month anniversary is bringing you some smiles along with the tears.

As you struggle through these first months without [name] by your side, I wish you strength to get through each day, wisdom to know what to do, and moments of peace. I will call soon to see how I can help.

As I look back on the months since [name's] death, I find myself hoping that I might be as fine and caring a person as [he/she] was. What an inspiration! I remember [him/her] today with a smile.

It's been over six months since [name] died. Most people probably expect you to be long over your grief. Yet you and I know better. We know that the reality is hitting home and, although the searing heat of pain may be diminishing, the sadness can ambush you at any time. Know that I am not one of those who expect you to be strong. I don't expect you to be "over it." I only hope that as each week passes you're able to feel whatever emotions arise and lean on those of us who care.

The one-year anniversary of [name's] death no doubt looms large in your thoughts. I imagine the past year has brought many tears interspersed with the everyday joys of life. It cannot be easy to turn the calendar and know that [name] is no longer only a phone call, e-mail, or visit away. Many grieving people report that the second year can be just as difficult, as the reality fully hits. I wish I could erase your grief and loneliness, but I cannot. What I can do is remind and reassure you of my constant friendship and willingness to listen. I will call you on Tuesday to see whether we can set up a time to have coffee together.

As you pass through the first anniversary of [name's] death, it must still seem impossible to imagine a future that doesn't include your beloved child. The circle of friends is moving on, growing up, and doing things your child won't do, and it hurts every time. At the same time, [name's] memory lives on in the hearts and minds of those who had the privilege of knowing [him/her], and they will be forever changed by that relationship. Those who loved [him/her] will never forget your child. As you move through the second year, I hope the pain eases and is balanced by a heart full of memories.

Do you remember a year ago when the pain was still so fresh? You've come so far since then! You've started forming new goals, and you've made important decisions to help you achieve them. I know it hasn't been easy, and at times, you've wanted to give up. I am inspired by your strength and resilience, and I'll do whatever I can to help you keep healing.

Today I wish you sunrise in the darkness, warmth in your heart, and peace in your soul. Remembering [name] and thinking of you.

On this, the [number] anniversary of [name]'s death, I offer a single rose in [his/her] memory.

Time passes and seasons change. Love remains forever. I'm thinking of you on this [number] anniversary.

The people you love forever change you, and you are a different person because [name] was in your life. That is a memory worth embracing.

One life can make such a difference. [Name's] certainly did. I remember with you.

Some people think you heal from grief by forgetting, by "putting this behind you now and getting on with life." They're wrong. You never forget. You take the love and the lessons with you as you move into a future that is enriched by [name]'s memory. So today, on this [number] anniversary, I toast [name] and all that [he/she] brought to life. May we all live well enough to honor [his/her] memory.

I was always impressed with [name] and the way [he/she] lived life. I miss that example. Yet in the time since [he/she] died, I have been equally impressed with you. This is an incredibly painful and lonely experience, but you keep putting one foot in front of the other, determined that you will heal and honor [name's] memory. I want to thank you for your fortitude and courage. I hope that when I inevitably face this situation myself, I'll cope as courageously as you have. In the meantime, I will continue to do what I can to companion you through this process.

A. A. Milne wrote, "There is something you must always remember: You are braver than you believe, stronger than you seem, and smarter than you think." In these months since [name's] death, you have proven Milne's assertions. I feel privileged to walk with you as you heal from your grief and move forward into the future.

There's an old saying: "Friends are those who know the song in my heart and sing it to me when I forget." In the midst of grief, it's hard to remember or sing your song. In these months since [name] died, I hope I've helped you not only remember your song but also to write new verses. I believe [name] would be proud of all you've done and of all you'll still accomplish.

I know you're getting anxious to [sell the house/move to the retirement community/other major decision involving a change in location or lifestyle]. Yet you've lost so much already. Perhaps the last thing you need is more loss on top of it. If you're willing to wait, I'll try to help you be patient, so you can make decisions when they're necessary and move wisely into the future. No matter what you decide, though, I'm on your side now and always.

Holidays or Marker Days

It must be surreal to look out your window at carolers, lights, trees, candles, and merriment. Your happy holidays this year are replaced by a range of emotions swirling like a dust storm through your heart. This holiday season will be a fog, and future holidays will never be the same again. In the midst of the craziness, I am here along with a host of other supportive people. I hope our care can offer you a measure of strength and sustenance to help you get through. I'll be checking in regularly. We'll do whatever we can to help. Keep breathing. You'll make it.

In this holiday season, your experience is almost an exact opposite of what is happening around you and what others are expecting from you. I hope you can let go of those expectations and do what makes sense for you. In the whirlwind that surrounds you, rely on those who get it and take the time you need. I'm here for you throughout this season and beyond.

When someone you love has died, the holidays are a time of intensely mixed emotions. There are moments when you enjoy yourself, smile, or even laugh. Yet [name's] absence is always with you, and those lighter moments will be mixed with times of deep sadness. In the midst of the craziness, it's especially important to take care of yourself and renew your spirit. I hope the enclosed gift certificate for a massage helps you do just that. Use it when you feel stressed and isolated or when you simply want to be pampered. My thoughts are with you throughout this time.

The upcoming holiday season is likely to be especially difficult as you go through familiar rituals without [name's] presence. I've also learned that it's common for everybody around you—possibly even your family members—to avoid mentioning [his/her] name. Or perhaps others will try to cheer you by saying things like "Be happy . . . it's what [he/she] would want for you." No doubt, [name] deeply wants your happiness, but I hope you can allow yourself the mixture of emotions that come unbidden this time of year—from gladness for the family you have to profound sadness that there is someone missing from the festivities. Allow each emotion its due, and you'll make it through. My phone and my home are always open when you need them, and I'll be in touch.

The holidays are a tough time when the one you love can't be here to share them. I hope the enclosed gift card for a massage provides a moment of respite from the craziness and helps renew your spirit.

For many grieving people, the anticipation leading up to a special day is worse than the actual day. As you approach [event or holiday], you may find yourself dreading the occasion and looking for a way out. The best wisdom I've heard is to plan how you want to mark the day. Some people want to be alone; others want to be with family or friends. Some want to be busy all day; others want quiet time to reflect, shed tears, and remember. Follow your own heart. Regardless of how you choose to spend the day, know that I hold you in my heart. I will be here as you continue to pass these milestone days and work toward a new future.

Today, on your birthday, you can't help but think about [name] and what it might be like if [he/she] were here. I remember two years ago when [name] was excited about the gift [he/she] had purchased for you. I'll never forget that twinkle in [his/her] eye. In spite of [his/her] physical absence, may you see just a bit of that twinkle today as you remember the gift that [he/she] was to your life.

It's your birthday [or (name's) birthday]. While many people who care may surround you, it will be painful not to have that one special person there. Even though it hurts, I hope you can open your heart enough to take in the love that others have for you, so you can let their care carry you through the day.

This is your first [birthday/Valentine's Day/Memorial Day/etc.] without [name]. It is sure to bring a mix of emotions as you remember and miss [him/her]. I'm remembering and missing [him/her], too. I'll call you later in the week so we can share our experiences of the day.

The upcoming [event] is sure to be difficult for you. You may be wondering how you will get through it. You may have to dig deep and tap into inner resources. Then remember the day is only twenty-four hours long. If you keep breathing and putting one foot in front of the other, it will pass and soon be behind you. Each time you make it through a tough situation, you're one step further along the path. As you heal, I'll do whatever I can to help you keep moving forward to find life again.

As we go through the holiday season, we'll all miss [name]. Yet no one will miss [him/her] more than you will. As you go through the ups and downs of these days, know that I'm in your corner. I'll do what I can to help you get through it and come out on the other side.

I won't wish you a happy holiday. I will wish you an honest holiday, where you're free to feel whatever you are feeling at the time without anyone else telling you otherwise. Do what seems right for you. Accept invitations, but feel free to change your mind or to leave early if you want. Be with others when it's comforting, but take time alone whenever you need it. No matter all the well-meaning advice, the path you take should be yours. I'll be in touch soon to check in and see how you're doing.

There are so many special days—anniversaries, birthdays, Valentine's Day, family gatherings. Do you sometimes feel that every time you turn around you have to steel yourself for something else? Yet each time, you make it through. You're surviving, and you will heal. Hang in there, and keep moving. I'm here for you.

These can be difficult days, and you must miss [him/her] a lot. I'm thinking of you, remembering with you, and pulling for you. Together, we'll keep moving forward day by day.

Today, I hope that you're able to remember not just [name's] death but also [his/her] life. Perhaps you can celebrate just a bit by treating yourself with this [chocolate/scones/other gift]. I'm thinking of you.

I remember [name] loved [flowers/tea/etc.]. On this day of memories and smiles mixed with loss and tears, I offer [flowers/tea/etc.] to you as a gift in [his/her] honor. May we both continue to live well enriched by [his/her] memory.

Death of a Sibling

The death of an older brother is the loss of a childhood "co-conspirator in adventure." While the schemes and shenanigans of childhood give way to the richer intimacy of adulthood, the simple bonds of childhood never go away. I hope that as you grieve [name's] death, you'll also remember the joy he brought to your life these many years. May you "conspire" to more adventures in memory of your brother.

When a younger sibling dies before you do, all seems wrong with the world. It's especially painful when it happens so abruptly. Thoughts of "Why not me?" are common. After all, you proudly protected this special person through thick and thin (even though there probably were some altercations from time to time). Though no one can replace [name], know that my heart is with you as you fondly recall your years together and grieve through the heartache that this separation brings.

When you lose an older [brother/sister], no matter what age, it's normal to feel especially vulnerable because a "protector" is gone. Though we may never mention the "protector" mantle past childhood, the security provided by an older sibling is always there. As you adjust to life without [his/her] physical presence, may you retain the bond of love you developed through the many years when your big [brother/sister] was always looking out for you.

May the memory of [name's] devotion to you as a big [brother/sister] sustain you even while you mourn [his/her] death and honor [him/her] with your own well-lived life.

It's been said that sisters are angels in disguise. While your sister may now be among the angels, the here and now is still a time of deep sadness because she has died. I hope you can surround yourself with friends and family who will help you remember the gift of [name's] life even while you mourn her death. I join my care to theirs so perhaps you may find some comfort in knowing you're not alone.

From what you told me, everyone who knew your [brother/sister] respected and loved [him/her]. Although [name] is no longer physically present with you and this reality brings untold sadness, [his/her] spirit lives on through the quiet and unassuming generosity [he/she] extended to so many. I honor that spirit this week by donating my time to [organization] in [his/her] memory, that [his/her] legacy of caring may continue.

Except for a parent, a [brother/sister] is likely one of the longest relationships we'll ever have. When the relationship ends through death, an essential link to life and love ends, too. Nobody will ever replace [name], but the bond you shared lives on in who you are because of [his/her] presence in your life. May that bond sustain you as you grieve. Know that I'm here for you.

I never had the joy of having a [sister/brother], and I can't fully understand what you must be going through right now. Yet I know from what you've told me that [name] will be especially remembered for [his/her] [particular quality]. May the happy memories you and [he/she] made together bring solace to help balance the sadness.

Death of a Child

Nothing, nothing is as hard as the death of one's own flesh and blood. It simply doesn't seem possible. If I thought words could provide the comfort you needed, surely I would write every day. Yet words fall short. Although I cannot say or do anything that will take away your pain, I want you to know that during this time of profound grief, I'll do whatever I can to walk through it with you and help you.

[Name] touched so many lives, in spite of the shortness of years, and [name's] memory lives on in the hearts and minds of those who had the privilege of knowing [him/her].

It must seem impossible to imagine a future that doesn't include your beloved child. [His/Her] circle of friends will move on, grow up, and do things your child won't, and it's bound to hurt every time. As you venture into your new reality, know that I'm here for you for the long term. I'll do what I can to help you remember, listen, and work to build a meaningful future. I begin by making a donation to [organization] as a living memorial to your child, so that others will continue to be touched by [his/her] legacy.

I've heard there is no grief as deep as after the death of a child. As I try to imagine even a little of what you're experiencing right now, I feel helpless. I only know I'm here for you as you go through it, to help guide you to wise decisions even when you can barely think, and to do whatever I can to make this difficult situation easier.

A child embodies our hopes and dreams and literally carries a bit of us into the future. When a child dies, those hopes and dreams die too. This makes your grief doubly hard, as you let go not only of [his/her] physical presence but of the vision you had for [his/her] life. I stand by you to help honor the memories of the past while building new hopes and dreams for a future that would make [name] proud.

As you cope with [name's] death, your pain will sometimes crash into you like tsunami waves, and you may feel you could drown in it. Other times, it will splash onto shore with the tide, pulling the sand out from under your feet. While I can't take away your grief, I hope our friendship can help you feel more anchored. As the storm passes, the future still awaits you. I'll do whatever I can to help you honor your child's memory by being here no matter what.

Death of a Parent

The death of a [mother/ father] is sometimes compared to the cutting of a kite string, setting you adrift. May [his/her] memory sustain you and [his/ her] example inspire you as you continue the flight through this world on which [he/she] first launched you. When you feel an old familiar tug of your "kite," you'll know you're never fully cut off from your [mother/father]'s love. That will endure forever.

A mother gives us breath itself, and when she dies, another arc in the circle of life is written upon our hearts and souls. As you grieve the death of your mother with your tears, may you also remember with your laughter and smiles the thousands of beautiful imprints she made on your life. My heart is with you.

Parents are our history, our anchor in time. Even if the relationship was problematic, when a [mother/ father] dies, our entire perspective changes. Although nothing can anchor you like your parents, I hope our friendship can help keep you grounded in love and care as you get accustomed to your new place in the world.

No matter what your age, when both of your parents have died, you are alone in a way you've never been before. You may even feel orphaned. As you take on the mantle of being the eldest generation in your family, I'll be here to stand with you, listen to you, and help you walk into a future that would make your parents proud.

Not everyone has a good relationship with [his/her] parents. Yet a parent's death has a deep impact on everyone. Now you face mixed emotions of sadness and relief, acknowledging the many years of hurt while also knowing it is impossible now to have the relationship with your [mother/father] you always hoped you could build. My friend, be assured that I'm here to listen if you want, to offer my help, and to support you as you try to build loving relationships and a worthy legacy to pass on to your own kids.

Terminal Illness

I am trying to imagine what the diagnosis of your [relative's] disease is like for you. As I do, I imagine that perhaps you are grateful for the years you've had with [him/her] fully present, yet simultaneously deeply sad and fearful for [his/her] diminishing state. It must be incredibly difficult. I offer you a listening ear, a willing researcher of resources, and an outstretched hand to help you and your family cope with this situation with as much grace and dignity as possible.

A serious diagnosis can imitate a dripping faucet. It's often simply there in the background, part of the fabric of your life that you try to live with or ignore. Other times, the ever-present dripping seems so loud and persistent that you think it'll drive you crazy. I wish there were a way to fix the faucet, but that's beyond my pay scale. Still, I'm by your side to do whatever I reasonably can to help, whether it's to curse the situation, drown out the dripping for a little while, or just sit with it. I'll call you early next week.

My sincerest hope for you is that [name's] treatment will result in a long period of remission. You still have dreams, hopes, energy, and goals that long to be fulfilled. I'll do what I can to help you prepare for any outcome, though, so you can concentrate on enjoying life together for as long as you have it.

Nothing ever prepares you to hear news like this diagnosis. As you look ahead into the blinding headlights, know that I'm here to help ensure you have the resources, help, and companionship you need to handle it.

I was saddened to hear that the prognosis now is bleak. It has to be painful and discouraging to know that, despite your incredible efforts to beat this, it may be a battle you can't win. As you consider your options for the immediate future, I understand that choosing to forgo further treatments isn't a sign that you're "giving up"; it's a courageous admission of reality and a decision that can allow you to live as fully as possible until you take your last breath. Remember too that even if there's nothing more that doctors can do to cure the illness, there is always something we can do for you. Caring people are here in various roles to help you live your remaining time and to help ensure you pass on a legacy of love. Know that I care, and I'm here to help you do both.

Death by Suicide
These can also be modified for drug overdose, murder, or other traumatic death

Suicide. It's hard even to say the word and almost impossible to attach it to someone you love. Often the experience is made worse because there are so many people who can't truly hear you, who make you feel ashamed or guilty, or who judge [name] for what [he/she] did. They may mean well, but they simply don't know any better. Rely instead on those who are willing to listen, to hold your pain, to shoulder your tears, and to embrace you where you are. I'd like to be one of those people for you. I'll check in with you on [date] to see if you'd welcome a visit or a conversation.

Although psychologists learn more about suicide all the time, you'll never be able to make sense of this. Even if you could, it wouldn't change what happened. It will be the biggest challenge of your life to work through [name's] death and heal. Because I value you as a person and as a friend, I'll stand by you through it all. I'll always listen to the truth, even when it's hard, and do what I can to help. I'll call you soon.

Every death brings a mixture of emotions, but death by suicide is particularly complex. The stigma is real, and the grief is profound. Emotions come swirling into your life with the power and intensity of a tornado, threatening to sweep you away. You may wonder whether you'll survive it. It can be immensely helpful to talk with others who understand as no one else can and to know you're not alone. I've enclosed information on an excellent support group and a competent counselor. Please don't face this alone. I'll continue to be in touch as a listening ear and a caring friend.

Suicide is such a baffling thing. What would cause such a bright, promising young person to take [his/her] own life? Could we have prevented it? Didn't [he/she] realize what it would do to the family? There are too many questions and too few answers, too much confusion and anger and too little consolation. As you work through the complex web of emotions and grief,

I hope I can be a safe and confidential ear. Know that I care deeply, and I will be in touch.

Nothing in your life can ever prepare you for a suicide. I imagine it still doesn't seem real, as if it's some kind of nightmare and you'll soon wake up. It certainly isn't the vision you had for [name] or for yourself. As you cope and find your way through this horrendously difficult time, I hold your broken heart in mine and I will do whatever I can to help you through.

Helen Keller said, "All that we love deeply becomes a part of us." Despite [name's] death by suicide, you clearly loved [him/her] deeply. The pain and grief you feel will take a long time and hard work to heal, and some of the love may seem overtaken by anger or guilt. In the end, though, the love is what will remain. [Name] will always have a place in your heart and in mine.

It is often helpful for grievers to talk to an objective person who doesn't have the baggage of family and who knows enough about grief to be a true sounding board and guide. This is especially true in cases of suicide, which are so much more complex. Right now, you are doing all you can to wake up in the morning, keep breathing, and survive this experience. As you do that, I am doing research on support groups and individual counselors who specialize in suicide, so you have them as an option for you and for the rest of the family. I will be in touch regularly, and I'll share the contact information for these resources. I hope that both will prove to be helpful for all of you in your arduous journey toward healing.

Longer Texts: Letters for Various Intervals

You may want to send a letter instead of a card, especially for friends you know well. The approximate timing is a guideline, although you can send any of these letters in the first two years following a death.

" *"Although our world is full of suffering, it is also full of the overcoming of it."* –HELEN KELLER

Letter for the First Two to Three Months

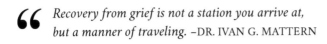 *Recovery from grief is not a station you arrive at, but a manner of traveling.* –DR. IVAN G. MATTERN

Dear [friend's name],

The funeral is over, and people have gone home. The harsh reality is sinking in. [Name] has died, and life will never be the same.

This can be a very hard time. You may find yourself feeling angry, empty, and lonely. People may not understand or may no longer want to hear your pain. You may be unsure of yourself or unable to concentrate or find stability. In fact, you may wonder whether you're going crazy.

First, I assure you that you are not going crazy. What you're experiencing is normal for a grieving person.

Grief is a process of creating a memory out of what can no longer be and moving into a future that is very different from the one you planned. It isn't easy, and it takes a long time. It's tempting to make it "go away" by keeping yourself too busy to think or feel. Yet grief is persistent, and it will force itself back into your life. It's best to deal with it as it comes to you, even though it may be raw and painful, so you continue to move forward.

Here are some things you can do:

Ignore people who say you "should" feel this or that, or you "should" put it behind you and get on with your life. Feel whatever you feel now; grieve on your own timetable.

Go to the cemetery if it's comforting; don't go if it isn't. Cry when you need to; laugh when you want. Express your emotions so they don't become trapped inside.

Forgive yourself for anything you regret, whether it was not saying goodbye, losing your temper, or wishing you'd done things differently. You did the best you could with what you had at the time; that's all anyone can expect. It's OK to forgive and let go.

Take care of yourself physically. Commit to getting enough sleep, eating healthy foods (with an occasional indulgence thrown in!), and exercising reasonably. Soak in a hot tub. Get a massage. Breathe deeply.

Find at least one person in whom you can honestly confide, and talk with him or her regularly.

Plan at least one enjoyable activity a week, and follow through even when you don't feel like it.

Make a list of the things you're thankful for and keep it handy. When you're having a bad day, it helps to remember that all of life isn't bad.

Reach out to someone else who's hurting or in need.

Read the wisdom of others. Use the library, the Internet, and bookstores to search out good resources. (*Note: If you can include a good book with this letter, it's even better.*)

Rely on your sense of spirituality in whatever way is meaningful to you, allowing your inner self to find consolation.

I will stay in regular contact with you because I know how hard grief can be. I also know that eventually the sun will shine in your heart and you will heal. I'll do whatever I can to help that happen.

I am here for you.

Letter at Four to Six Months

 There is a sacredness in tears. They are not the mark of weakness but of power. They speak more eloquently than ten thousand tongues. They are messengers of overwhelming grief, of deep contrition, and of unspeakable love. –WASHINGTON IRVING

Dear [friend's name],

By now, you've probably experienced the "roller coaster effect" of grief. Just when you feel you're healing—you have more energy, you feel lighter than before, and you're relieved to be finally through the worst—suddenly you spiral down again.

These unwelcome events can be triggered by seeing someone who looks like [name] or hearing a certain song, or there may be no discernible trigger at all. You just know you were feeling better, and now you're feeling lousy again. Many people begin to wonder whether they're healing at all, whether they will ever recover, or whether they're doomed to grinding pain for the rest of their lives.

I hope it helps you to know that you're healing in a normal and expected way. Healing is not a linear process, where you feel incrementally better until you completely heal. It's more like a roller coaster, going up and down repeatedly. Another analogy sometimes used is an onion—you deal with continual layers of grief, each one getting closer to the center of your pain and plunging you temporarily back into the abyss.

Studies have shown that it's extremely common to experience a serious "down time" starting anywhere from four to nine months after someone you love dies. The numbness or shock has worn off, and reality stares you squarely in the face. It is a stressful and often emotional period.

When you experience this, don't give up. Rather than regressing, you're healing a little bit deeper. Each time you go through a difficult period, face a holiday, or handle a painful situation, you get stronger. Each time you spiral down, the pain you endure is stretching you and helping you heal. You are not going back to ground zero. It's more like two steps forward and one back, then three steps forward and one or two back. You are progressing, actually getting somewhere; the process of grief just doesn't happen in a straight line.

Keep your hope alive, even when it's just barely flickering. Over time, the world will brighten for you again, you'll notice yourself smiling more and crying less, and the intensity of your grief will decrease. Life is still a marvelous gift, and you have a lot of living to do. I'll do whatever I can to support you in your grief journey and help you work toward healing.

I am here for you.

Letter at Seven to Nine Months

> 66 *I walked a mile with pleasure; she chattered all the way,*
> *But left me none the wiser for all she had to say.*
> *I walked a mile with sorrow; And ne'er a word said she;*
> *But, oh, the things I learned from her when sorrow walked with me!*
> –ROBERT BROWNING HAMILTOn

Dear [friend's name],

In some ways, it seems like just yesterday that [name] died. In other ways, it seems like an eternity.

Over time, many grieving people find themselves thinking about things that were left unresolved. One widow never got to say goodbye to her husband before he died. One man's last words to his son were angry. A woman knew she and her sister had hurt each other, but they didn't have time to work it out before her sister died in an accident.

One technique many grievers find helpful is writing a letter to their deceased loved one. You can say everything you need to say, tell of your pain now, acknowledge any pain you caused, forgive and ask for forgiveness. Hold nothing back. Then do what makes sense with the letter. You can bury it at the gravesite, burn it in a fireplace, tear it into little shreds, store it in a memory box, or whatever else feels right to you.

Many grieving people also find it helpful to keep a journal. You don't have to be an experienced writer. Just buy a notebook and make an entry every day. Spell out your anger, fear, struggles, insights, and joys, knowing that no one else ever has to read it. Your notebook is constantly available as a safe, accessible outlet for your experience. In fact, some mourners find it helpful to write just before bed, to prevent waking up in the middle of the night full of unexpressed thoughts or feelings. As an added bonus, when you get discouraged and think you haven't made any progress, you can look back and see how far you've come.

Another tip that helps many people is to make at least one new beginning. Learn a new hobby, take a class that interests you, plan a trip to a new location, or grow plants you've never grown before. Choose an activity you can relish and anticipate, and do it regularly.

You may or may not find these techniques useful. I offer them as simple suggestions because they've helped others who have lost loved ones. Whether you use these ideas or others, I am here to help you find that life is still worth living, that there is much to explore and learn, and that in spite of the trials and pain, this world is still a fascinating and wonderful place. Your life will never be the same, but it can be good again.

I'll call you soon.

Letter at Eleven Months

 These, then, are my last words to you: Be not afraid of life. Believe that life is worth living, and your belief will help create the fact. –WILLIAM JAMES

Dear [friend's name],

Though it hardly seems possible, soon it will be a year since [name] died. This first anniversary is usually a deeply sensitive time. Be aware of "anniversary anxiety," where dreadful anticipation causes the days before the anniversary to be more stressful than the day itself. Be assured that although the day marks a painful milestone, it will pass, and you will make it through.

It can be helpful to plan what you want to do that day. Here are a few ideas that have worked for others. Gather with significant people at your home to remember, cry, hug, and eat together. Go out for part or all of the day. If it's a workday, you may want to maintain that part of your normal routine, or perhaps you wish to just be alone. It may be comforting to visit the cemetery or attend services at your church. There is no "right" way to observe the anniversary. Decide what you need and want to do, and then let others know your wishes so they don't surprise you with something you don't want.

The anniversary is also a good time to take stock of the last twelve months. You made it through all the "firsts"—the first holiday season, the first birthday, etc.—and you survived. You grew and changed as a person, becoming more appreciative, aware, tolerant, and compassionate. In spite of the pain you still feel, you healed tremendously and are less likely to take life or relationships for granted.

Your grief isn't resolved yet. The second year will carry its own type of pain as the reality fully sets in. You'll encounter people who say, "Surely you're healed by now," or "It's been a whole year—why do you still cry?" They'll tell you to put it behind you and get on with life. They simply don't understand that, in many ways, grief is a lifelong process. It won't continue to be as fresh or raw, and your sad times will become less frequent and less intense until they're only sporadic. Yet you'll never forget someone you loved this much. You'll never stop missing them or wondering what life would be like if they were still alive. For the rest of your life, even if you haven't cried in years, there will be times when you are ambushed and the tears will flow again.

Try to trust yourself and your gradual healing process more than you listen to well-meaning but uninformed people. Remember in ways that make sense to you, even if others don't understand. I will be here to support you as your journey toward peace and healing continues through the coming year.

Letter at Fourteen to Fifteen Months

 Lost irreversibly in objective time, the person is present in a new form within one's mind and heart, tenderly present in inner time without the pain and bitterness of death. And once the loved one has been accepted in this way, he or she can never again be forcefully removed.
–R.C. CANTOR

Dear [friend's name],

This isn't a particular anniversary or marker day, but I wanted to let you know that even though it has been more than a year since [name] died, I still remember with you.

Sometimes people think that to remember a person you have to visualize every detail of their physical appearance. Those people panic, as details inevitably get fuzzy.

Instead, realize that the most important memory you have of [name] lies within. You are a different person because [he/she] loved you, and no one can ever take that away. You will forever carry with you all that [name] meant to you, all that [he/she] taught you, and all that you've become as a result. These are the memories worth hanging onto, even as you create new tomorrows.

You can honor [name] by choosing to live as fully and vibrantly as you can, enriched by [his/her] memory.

I care about you so much. I am here for you, so together we can remember but continue to move forward.

Articles for Grieving Friends and Family

You may wish to send articles to some of the grievers you care about, especially if they are struggling with a particular aspect of their grief. These are possibilities to consider. Reading through them may also increase your personal understanding of the grief experience.

Anything and Everything, Except the Obvious

How often does it happen? You get together with family or friends, and you're having a good time. Yet after a while, you notice that people are talking about everything and everyone *except* the person who died, even when it would be natural to include something about him or her in the conversation. They all tiptoe around it and avoid even mentioning the person's name. Why is everyone so afraid?

The truth is, they are well meaning but uninformed. They are afraid that if they say the name, they will make you sad or spoil your evening. They think it is their job to cheer you up or take your mind off the reality.

They don't realize it is not their job to "fix it." They can't take your grief away anyway: the loss is always in your mind, no matter how hard others try to move it away. Nor do they realize how much you long to hear the name, how badly you want to know that someone besides you remembers, or how hungry you are for the stories and memories they could share.

They can be much more comforting if they can acknowledge and accept your sadness, give you an understanding smile or a hug, or even cry with you. Shared grief diminishes, but grief that is repressed or denied festers inside until it finds a way to come out.

Besides, tears are healthy. Despite our fears to the contrary, no one in the history of the world has ever started crying and not been able to stop. Most people report feeling relieved, freed, or even cleansed after a good cry. In addition, tears contain physiological chemicals that relieve stress; we are supposed to cry when we are sad.

So what can you do when people are afraid to say the name? The easiest thing is to say the name yourself. Bring up a story or a memory that involves your spouse whenever it seems to fit. That gives others permission to say the name too.

You can even address the issue explicitly, saying, "You know, sometimes people are afraid to mention the name for fear of making me sad. Yet I love to hear it and to share in your stories and memories. Please don't be afraid."

If you do start to cry, say something like, "Don't worry. You did not make me cry. The tears are there anyway, and every once in a while they spill over. It's okay. Please don't let my tears make you stop talking about your memories. I love to know that someone else remembers too."

You will still find that some people are uncomfortable with your grief and sadness. In their presence, you may have to go along with the illusion that you are happy and that everything is fine. There will be others, though, with whom you can freely share whatever you are experiencing. Friends who can hear you, hug you, cry with you, and walk through grief with you are priceless treasures. With them, you can truly have a good time.

Chasing after Closure

I keep reading in the newspapers about survivors of tragedy or death seeking "closure." Yet no one really defines what closure means, whether it is possible, or how to get there.

For many in our society, closure means leaving grief behind, a milestone usually expected within a matter of weeks or months. Closure means being "normal": getting back to your old self and no longer crying or being affected by the death. It means "moving on with life" and leaving the past behind, even to the extent of forgetting it or ignoring it. For those of us who have experienced death, this kind of closure is not only impossible but also indeed undesirable.

Closure, if one even chooses to use the term, is more of a process than a defined moment. The initial part of closure is accepting the reality. At first, we keep hoping or wishing that it weren't true. We expect our loved one to walk through the door. We wait for someone to tell us it was all a huge mistake. We just can't accept that this person has died, that we will never physically be together again on earth, or that we will not hear the voice, feel the hug, or get the person's input on a tough decision. Usually, it takes weeks or even months for the reality to finally sink in. We come to know, in both our heads and in our hearts, that our loved one has died and is not coming back. We still don't like it, but we accept it as true.

As the reality sinks in, we can more actively heal. We begin making decisions and start to envision a life different from what we had planned before, a life in which we no longer expect our loved one to be there. We grow, struggle, cry, and change. We form fresh goals. We face our loneliness. We feel the pain and loss, but except for short periods, we are not crippled by it. We also make a shift in memory. Memories of our loved one, rather than being painful as they were at first, sometimes make us smile or even laugh.

This healing phase takes a long time, and it involves a lot of back-and-forthing. We alternate between tears and joy, fears and confidence, and despair and hope. We take two steps forward and one step back. We wonder whether we'll ever be truly happy again and often doubt that we will.

Eventually, we realize we are taking the past, with all its pain and pleasure, into a new tomorrow. We never forget, and in fact, we carry our beloved with us; he or she is forever a cherished part of who we are. We are changed by the experience of having loved this person, by the knowledge of life's transience, and by grief itself. We become different and hopefully better—more compassionate, more appreciative, more tolerant—people. We fully embrace life again, connecting, laughing, and loving with a full heart.

Still, there is no point of "final closure," no point at which you can say, "Ah, now I have finally completed my grief." Or "Yes, now I have healed." Or "I will never miss him again, or wonder what life would be like if he were still alive." There is no point at which you will never cry again, although as time goes on, the tears are bittersweet and less common. Healing is a lifelong process, one in which you often don't even realize you are healing until you look back and see how far you've come.

Closure? I don't think so. Acceptance—yes. Peace—yes. Hope—definitely. Putting a period behind the final sentence and closing the book on it? No, life and love are much too complex for that. The story does not end; instead, it awaits the next chapter.

The Starting Point—Filling the Emptiness

Dave Barry wrote, "My psychologist tells me it is more satisfying to finish what I've started. He's right. Today I've finished two bags of M&M's and a chocolate cake, and I feel better already." If you're a person who regularly goes for a "chocolate fix," this quote could make you chuckle. However, it also points out our love/hate relationship with food, especially when we're grieving.

When you feel that familiar gnawing pain in your gut—that unsettled empty void—it's so easy to go for the comfort foods: ice cream, chocolate, biscuits and gravy, a juicy steak, or anything else that seems like it will "fill up" the emptiness or "stuff down" those pesky emotions that keep welling up. Perhaps instead you go for a glass of wine (or two or three), a few beers, or a stiff martini. Another common alternative is drowning out the pain with absorbing work, intense exercise, endless Internet searches and YouTube videos, or an overly busy schedule.

Unfortunately, none of these things works for long. You aren't really longing for chocolate, and you're not hungry for food. Alcohol only covers up the pain temporarily. After the work or the frenzied activity is done, the grief awaits you.

Pushing down the grief, denying it, or covering it up will not make it go away. In fact, suppressed grief simply festers inside and waits for an opportunity to show itself. It may come out in physical ways—headaches, neck aches, backaches, or stomachaches. It may come out in psychological ways like outbursts of anger, impatience with people who don't deserve it, depression, or suicidal thoughts. Perhaps saddest—because so much repressed grief and hurt lurks inside—is a life that is never truly joyful again or a person who has an inability to love deeply again.

It is certainly a lot more difficult to confront the loss than to indulge in a hot fudge sundae. Yet, to heal, you need to avoid that temptation to cover it up, push it down, deny its existence, or pretend it is something that it's not. Instead, we hope you can find the courage to express the sadness: remember your beloved, tell someone about the void, cry whenever you feel the need, write, pound nails, or find some other way to express and process what you're experiencing.

When you face the pain honestly and work through it with the help of supportive people, you will eventually heal. You may also find that as you quit substituting false fixes, a hot fudge sundae can be even more enjoyable because it's a treat and not a leaky bandage.

Can you trust the process more than you trust your favorite comfort foods? Can you avoid the phony, temporary, illusive solutions in favor of those that will bring lasting healing and happiness? And along the way, don't forget that you can still have a few M&M's.

Grieve with Hope

Recently, a man wrote of the crisis he went through when he turned fifty. He realized his life might be half over (or more), yet there was so much he still wanted to do and experience. He started to feel the preciousness of time and the compulsion to make the most of whatever he had left. It caused him to re-evaluate how he spent his time, what he spent his money on, and which things and people were truly important in his life. He read books, pondered, and finally made some decisions that, in big and small ways, changed the way he lived.

When his wife was diagnosed with cancer and died of it eight years later, he was awash in grief. He couldn't imagine life without her: his emotions seemed out of control, and he wanted her back. Gradually, as he came to accept the fact that he couldn't have her back and that her death was now a permanent fixture of his life, he also realized that he was still alive.

He realized anew that life is transient and unpredictable: he could have many years left, or he could get a bad diagnosis next week. Even more powerfully than his fiftieth birthday had, his wife's death woke him up to the precious-ness of time and the unknown amount he has left.

Prompted by this knowledge, he is once again in the process of re-evaluating his life, although this time without her by his side. He is thinking hard about what gives him enjoyment, what gifts he can share with others, how he can make a difference and live with meaning, who and what are truly important, where he spends money, and how he spends the minutes of his day.

Everything has changed for him, and he is doing his best to consciously, reflectively, and prayerfully change with it. He wants to carry his wife's love with him and find ways to give that love to others on her behalf. Knowing he may have much or only a little time left, he wants to honor his wife by living his own life as fully as possible.

This is easier said than done, and some days he just wants to hide in bed or die himself. Yet he remembers her, and it keeps him putting one foot in front of the other. It keeps him talking to supportive people so he can process his grief, and it keeps him searching for new goals in his life. He grieves with hope.

No matter who or what you have lost, you are still alive. There can be joy and happiness ahead if you choose it. The pain is real and intense, but heal-ing is possible. Each morning, try to make one more small decision for life. Grieve, but with hope.

How to Handle Your Fears after the Death of a Spouse

> *We have the opportunity to face what is there—ourselves . . . We will find that we're less than we wish, as imperfect as we feared. But having faced that . . . we free ourselves. New energies will be released within the creative part of us, the part that wants to grow, the part that is ready to reach beyond . . . We begin to feel less anguish and more comfort, less threat and more promise. The promise is that by living fully our aloneness, we can become more whole. We can become more who we were meant to be.* –JAMES MILLER, *A Pilgrimage Through Grief*

"For so long I experienced life as John and Amy, as Mr. and Mrs. Now I am just Amy. Amy alone. No John by my side. And I am terrified."

I wrote this journal entry about two weeks after another car slammed broadside into my husband's, killing him instantly. In that moment, death slammed broadside into my life, and I had to learn to let go of the one person I thought I could never live without. I felt many things: anxiety, sadness, gratitude, loneliness, anger, and more. As I looked ahead, though, there was one overriding emotion: fear. I didn't know where to turn or who to count on. I felt unable to make decisions, incapable of even the simplest tasks.

I have since learned that fear, like grief, need not dominate your life or last forever. When we express and honestly deal with fears, they eventually resolve, leaving hope for peace, healing, and even joy.

So let's look at some fears that come with the territory and share suggestions for coping. Although your grief is individual and unique, perhaps some of these tips will work for you.

Build a New Normal

Three months after John's death, I said to a friend, "I'm scared to look ahead. When those two cars hit, all our plans and dreams evaporated, and there is nothing left. My entire future got wiped out in an instant."

My friend wisely said, "No, Amy, your future was not wiped out. John's was, at least on this earth. You still have a future; it's just going to be very different than you thought." Her words pierced through the fog. She was right.

The next evening, I looked back at goals I'd written in my journal. Some were directly related to John, but others were not. I wanted to vacation at the ocean, audition for the community theater, and work with the church youth group. I dreamed of taking voice lessons and someday publishing a book. There were still goals I could reach and things I could do, if I so chose. I could never go "back to normal"—that "normal" would never exist again. Yet perhaps I could build a "new normal" that fit me. It wouldn't be the same without John, but for the first time, I dared to think that maybe it could still be good. There was some continuity. Not all was gone. I did indeed have a future.

Face the Emotions

C.S. Lewis wrote, "No one ever told me that grief felt so like fear." Because it is scary to confront grief, many widowed people avoid solitude like the plague. They obey the "standard wisdom" that says you should keep busy and not think about it. Granted, a certain amount of busyness is a good thing. It is healthy to grieve in spurts, allowing yourself time to relax, to breathe, and even to laugh. Yet we need balance because grief doesn't go away until you deal with your emotions.

Take time to name and express your feelings. I wrote in a journal every night. Sometimes I sat on the "pity pot" temporarily, feeling sorry for myself, whining, or throwing an old-fashioned temper tantrum on the floor. Perhaps you prefer to pound nails into wood. You can sketch, scribble, or use finger paints. Some people make something out of clay or Play-Doh and then decide whether to smash it or keep it. None of this has to be "good," and no one ever has to see it. It just has to get the emotions out.

Through it all, go ahead and cry. It is common to fear that once you start crying, you won't be able to stop. But that has never happened in the history of humankind. You'll be OK. In fact, you'll be more OK than before. There are physiological chemicals in tears that relieve stress.

Finally, when your emotions are spent for now, do something comforting. I loved to light candles and soak in a hot bath. Perhaps you'd like to eat fresh popcorn or listen to classical music. Some people take comfort in a cup of tea, a brisk walk or swim, or simply standing outside and breathing deeply of the fresh air. It feels good and helps restore some of the energy that grief siphons off.

Find New Friends

Many widowed people rightly fear that they no longer fit into their social circles. If you have known a couple for a long time, they may remain good friends, providing stability even as others fall away. For the most part, though, your life has changed, and your network of friends eventually reflects that fact. You need to build new connections, particularly among unmarried people.

The most comfortable relationships, especially initially, are with other widowed people. After all, they understand your experience. Check your place of worship, hospice, or hospital for support groups. It takes courage to attend, but it is well worth it. The people there will nod their heads and affirm your feelings; they've been there too. It provides a nonthreatening way to create new support and friendship networks. Like you, most of them are looking for someone to have coffee with, a group to see a movie with, or a phone number they can call when it's a rough day.

Be Safe

Everyone who lives alone knows that houses creak and groan, especially in the middle of the night. Movies and TV shows play off the horror of confronting a lunatic with a weapon. Rather than being overcome by fear, take reasonable steps to increase your safety. If you don't have one, install a home alarm. Have outside lights on motion sensors. Always lock doors, regardless of whether you're home. Ensure that windows are secure and that sliding doors have security bars.

Some people turn on a TV to have a voice in the house, or they play music that provides noise and relaxes them at the same time. Keep pepper spray on your nightstand and have another on your keychain to carry with you.

You may want to take a self-defense class at a local community college or park district. Practicing the techniques is good exercise, and interacting with other people is good for your spirit. It will also help you regain a sense of strength and control.

Discover Yourself

So much of your identity and routine were intertwined with your spouse that it's hard to know who you are by yourself. You can feel vulnerable and exposed.

If you are open, though, you may begin to discover the freedom and adventure of being on your own. For instance, one woman's husband would only eat butter pecan ice cream, so that's all she ever bought. After he died, she wanted to find the ice cream she liked best. She discovered two favorites: mint chocolate chip and rocky road. She still occasionally has butter pecan in memory of her husband, but now she knows something about herself she didn't know before. It was one small step in discovering her new identity.

It is amazing to find out how many things you can do. I learned how to mow the lawn and do simple plumbing repairs. I got a device to help open tight jar lids. I painted the bedroom a different color. For areas where I didn't feel competent, I got help. For instance, I asked friends until I found a good handyman and a trustworthy financial advisor.

As I learned and grew, I became stronger and more confident in myself. Of course, I still missed John, wished he were there, and sometimes resented being alone. But I also came to know I could survive without him and perhaps one day even enjoy life again.

Imagine the Worst

It may seem counterintuitive, but sometimes the most helpful way to handle fears is to imagine the worst that could possibly happen and then decide whether you could survive it. What is the worst scenario, for instance, if you don't have enough money to keep your house?

Even though you don't want to, could you survive if you had to get an apartment or move in with a grown child? Chances are good that no matter the consequences of your fears, you would still be OK if the worst happened. That knowledge can take away some of fear's power. You can cope. You can go on. You can survive.

Heal

Healing takes longer than you imagine. Sometimes you take three steps forward and two steps back. For many people, the second year is as hard as the first, just in different ways. But gradually, the memories bring smiles instead of tears, and you take the past with you into a new tomorrow. You never forget; you carry your beloved with you forever as a cherished part of who you are, yet you grow and become a more compassionate, appreciative, and tolerant person. As you keep facing your fears, you will learn to embrace life again, connecting, laughing, and loving with a full heart.

Keeping Busy

I can't count the number of times I've asked people how they cope with grief and they say, "Well, I keep myself busy."

Keeping busy can be a good thing. We all need to have a purpose, a reason to get out of bed in the morning. We all have gifts and talents to share, and we are called to offer them to others. We all need enough money to live, and most of the time staying employed makes that possible.

However, you need to make sure that keeping busy doesn't become the excuse that keeps you from grieving. It is easy to fill every hour with activity to avoid facing the fact that you are alone. It is easy to wear yourself out so thoroughly that you are too exhausted to think about what has happened.

Our society feeds the tendencies to stay busy because we value productivity and deny pain. After a tragedy, you are expected to pick yourself up and move on. You are told not to be a burden and not to bring everybody else down. You are told that it's time you put this behind you and get on with life.

Give yourself permission to ignore society. Give yourself plenty of time and space to grieve. Cry until you think you can't cry any more. Go ahead and feel lonely. Feel sorry for yourself for a while. Scream and throw a temper tantrum.

Be angry. Be sad. Be grateful. Recognize and deal with all those emotions that come tumbling out.

Why should you let yourself feel all this pain? Otherwise, you will never truly heal. Grief unexpressed does not go away. It lurks just under the surface, waiting to rear its ugly head when you least expect it. Your emotions are less controllable, so you find yourself reacting to things in ways that are entirely out of proportion. You may sob over distant deaths or even cry over a game show. The more you try to hold in all the pain, the more determined it is to come out. You can even make yourself physically sick by refusing to face your grief.

Is it hard to allow the pain? Yes. You may wish to take advantage of a support group so you can share your struggle. Perhaps you prefer to read the stories of others so you gain their wisdom and advice. You may choose quieter activities like writing, playing music, or drawing your experience. You may choose physical activities like sports, running, dancing, or stomping your feet.

It is good to be busy—to have goals and purpose in your life. It is also good to help yourself heal, so you can better enjoy the life you have now. Happiness and satisfaction are still possible, especially if you don't use the busyness of life to avoid doing the things that can help you find them.

The Changing Palette

John Paul Floyd was six years old—a carefree, loving boy. He was playing with his brother David in the front yard of their home when, without warning, a car jumped the curb and struck the two boys. David was injured, and John Paul was killed. Thus began the nightmare for the Floyd family.

Gregory Floyd, the boys' father, described his grief journey in a wonderful book entitled *A Grief Unveiled*. He also helped create videos on grief and gave talks and presentations. One of his images for the grief process may be particularly helpful to you.

Greg reported that even in the beginning, when the grief is most intense and the pain is searing, there are sometimes brief moments of joy. Some little thing makes you smile. Someone unexpectedly gives you a hug when you most need it. You momentarily lose yourself in a movie or a show, and you laugh out loud.

Those moments can bring instant guilt. "How can I be happy when this person I love just died?" You may feel you are being disloyal to the person's memory when you don't remain in your grief. You may even feel that you aren't ready to let go of the pain because the pain is your closest connection to the one who died: if the pain is diminishing, perhaps the connection is diminishing.

Yet grieving well does not mean being sad every second of every day. We need those little breaks and rays of sunshine to survive. Greg advised that we should treasure those moments of joy because they sustain us. He called them the "bright splashes of color on the gray palette of grief."

Don't worry. You will neither lose your grief nor forget your loved one if you smile occasionally. Those smiles are the necessary break in the bleakness, the glimmer of hope that perhaps there can still be happiness in life.

As you continue to heal, those "good" times become more frequent and more intense, while the bad times become less frequent and less intense. For instance, one day you realize that you cried only for a half-hour that day. Then you realize you haven't cried in three days. Eventually, you pass the milestone where you haven't cried in weeks. It takes a long time, and the balance shifts back and forth on a regular basis.

Finally, you reach a point where the pain of grief does not define you. Your palette has changed. The joy is no longer the bright splash of color on the gray palette of grief. Instead, the pain becomes the gray splash of color on the bright palette of life.

You never totally lose the gray. You will experience grief bursts or "ambushes" for as long as you live. You will never stop missing the one you so loved or wondering what life would be like if he or she were still alive. Yet you don't have to live your life in gray tones. There is still exuberant color waiting for you, unbridled joy to experience, new things to learn, loving friends to meet, and a promising future to rebuild.

It is a long process to move from a gray palette to a colored one. Start by accepting those splashes of color and treasuring each one as a gift. Allow yourself whatever joy you can without guilt or regret. After all, your best memorial to the ones who died is to live as fully and colorfully as possible, enriched by their memory.

The Fog of Grief: A Widow's Essay

This morning, it was so foggy I could barely see across the street. People appeared out of nowhere, walked by, and disappeared again. Like a scene from a horror movie, it was an uncertain, claustrophobic, potentially dangerous world.

Ah, but then the sun fought through. I can see the old tree, its barren branches framing a plane in the distance. More distant still are wispy clouds. My world now encompasses thousands of people—flying, driving, and working. Everything looks and feels entirely different. Of course, the world has not substantially changed since this morning. It is my perception—the depth and clarity of my vision—that makes it appear so.

Likewise, when my husband died, the world closed in. The sunshine of our dreams was forever shrouded, and my world went gray and cold. I was blinded by pain—by the loss of one I held so dear. I felt cut off, empty, and surrounded by swirling shadows, unable to envision a future.

About six weeks after his death, I told a friend that my entire future was wiped out in an instant. She said, "No, your future wasn't wiped out. His was. You still have a future; it will just be a much different future than you had planned."

Her words struck hard. I wasn't allowing myself to see the future because I didn't want it to exist without him. Yet I didn't want to live in a dismal fog for the rest of my life. I did indeed have a future; it was my choice to step into it.

Burning away the fog was hard work and took a long, long time. Slowly, my future emerged from the haze and began taking shape. Eventually, as the light poked through, I stepped tentatively out of the mist, and it felt good.

I know now that the world does not disappear when death occurs. It is only my perception—the depth and clarity of my vision—that makes it seem so. Though the sun may be veiled, it is not extinguished. The future may be shrouded, but it still exists, waiting to be discovered. Life may seem empty, but joy, surprises, and delight yet abound. Beyond the murkiness lie new possibilities, if only we have eyes to see and courage to follow our sight.

The Greatest Gift

 Some people run away from grief, go on world cruises or move to another house or another town. But they do not escape, I think. The memories, unbidden, spring into their minds, scattered perhaps over the years, but always there. There is, maybe, something to be said for facing them all deliberately and straightaway . . . .

I would not run away from grief; and I would not try to hold onto it when—if, unbelievably—it passed. –SHELDON VANAUKEN, *A Severe Mercy*

It is a universal human experience: when something good happens, we want to remember it. How often have we heard (or said), "I will never forget this day as long as I live," or "I will always remember what you have done for me?" The desire to remember—to immortalize certain people or events—takes on extreme importance when someone you love dies.

I was widowed at the age of twenty-five when my husband John was killed in a car accident. People flooded the wake and funeral, and it was gratifying to know he had made a difference to so many. Still, the rest of the world took no notice. I was appalled as I rode to the cemetery and saw people gardening, buying groceries, and proceeding with their normal routines. I felt that John deserved five minutes of silent prayer, flags lowered to half-mast, schools canceled for the day, or some recognition of his loving, generous life. I instantly understood why survivors build memorials to the deceased.

In the awful time following the funeral, there were many ways to memorialize John. I made dozens of reprints of photographs and distributed them to anyone who was interested. His watch, scrapbook, and other mementos became precious treasures. Because John had worked with the youth in our town, a scholarship fund was started in his name, and enough money was contributed to make a yearly award to a graduating senior. I gave many of John's clothes to family and friends so they could have a visual reminder of him. I kept the rest of his clothes in a special drawer, sometimes wearing one item or just holding it, stroking it, remembering, and crying.

I struggled to conceive of spending my life without John. It made me more determined than ever to remember. I concentrated on his laugh, his eyes, his hands, and his walk. When I couldn't picture a scene with absolute clarity, I panicked. I wanted him to stay "alive," and my mind refused to cooperate.

Despite my efforts, he could never again be alive for me. My fuzzy recollections were simply reminders of that fact.

It took much pain and tremendous struggle, but I began to heal. Little by little, I built a life for myself apart from John. Piece by piece, I parted with the clothes that had been so precious. I still have some physical reminders of John, but the ways of remembering that were so important to me in those first two or three years have lost their extreme significance now. I replaced them with new ways of remembering and with a new understanding of what it means to remember.

In its simplest form, remembering means merely "bringing again to mind." As I realized I could no longer bring aspects of John to mind with clarity, I feared that I was forgetting him. Yet there is a deeper meaning to remembering. A "member" is a part of the whole. "Remembering" entails recalling the important aspects and people of my past and assimilating them into my being. My most indelible "memory" of John, then, is not the physical details. The most indelible memory I carry is myself—who I was and who I have become as a result of his influence in my life. Other people were also permanently affected by knowing him. There is no fame, wealth, power, or status in that; yet it is the most important contribution that any of us can make. The world—my world—is a better place because of John.

My lessons did not stop with John's life. His death is undoubtedly the most heart-wrenching, exhausting, and difficult thing that ever happened to me. Yet, as a consequence, I am more compassionate and empathetic. I have a clearer sense of my strengths and weaknesses. I am more tolerant of others and their limitations. My faith is stronger and more deeply rooted. I am more appreciative and loving.

I rarely take people, things, or life itself for granted because I am aware in my innermost being of the swiftness with which it can disappear. I am an optimist. I believe in the ultimate goodness of life and in the power of joint human and divine effort to transform senseless tragedy into blessing. The grief experience has changed the way I live, and the changes have been positive.

I remember feeling that I would never be truly happy again. Thankfully, I was wrong. I am happy now, delighted with life and living it vibrantly. I have been to hell and back, I was transformed by my experience, and I am better for it. That is a memory worth hanging on to.

Twelve Steps for Healthy Grieving

You never thought it would happen to you. Yet here you are, grieving and in pain. It is so tempting to ignore the emotions of grief because they hurt so deeply. Yet unresolved grief is like buried toxic waste: although it isn't evident on the surface, it keeps finding ways to come up, often with unpleasant consequences. It may manifest as headaches or stomachaches, as outbursts of anger or impatience against people who don't deserve it, as depression or suicidal thoughts, or as paranoia or withdrawal from life. It may make you reluctant to get close to another person, or it may make you afraid to love.

1. The truth is this: Nothing can simply make your grief go away. You must acknowledge, face, and resolve your grief.

2. This list of suggestions for healthy ways to cope with grief may be helpful as you follow your own path to healing.

3. Expect to recover. Affirm that you will be able to make it and that the resources you need are there if you want them.

4. Set long-range goals for things you eventually would like to have or do. Allow yourself to dream, even if it seems crazy.

5. Do short-term things: go to a movie, soak in a bath, read a good book—whatever comforts you and brings some relief.

6. Never go to sleep without breathing deeply, smiling at least once, and being thankful for what you still have.

7. Keep in touch with your feelings as you ride the roller coaster of up and down, round and round, and back and forth. All grief gets "reworked." You go through it repeatedly, yet you are always moving forward.

8. Find ways to express your emotions. Write in a private journal, pound nails into wood, paint, sculpt, throw a tennis ball against a wall vigorously, write a letter to the one who died or left you, and do what seems right with it (bury it at the gravesite, tear it up, burn it, keep it in a memory box, etc.).

9. Find at least one person you can talk to honestly and from the heart. If possible, also find a good support group.

10. Read as much as you can. There is great wisdom in the experience of others.

11. Ask for and give forgiveness, whether to the person who died, God, or those still living. None of us are perfect people; we are just people. Accept your imperfections and limitations, and be willing to ask forgiveness for whatever you feel you did wrong or for whatever you feel you didn't do. Work through the experiences of hurt and anger until you can offer forgiveness in return. Lack of forgiveness shackles your heart, mind, and body. Forgiveness sets you free.

12. Remember the past, fondly and often, but don't live in the past. There is no future in that.

13. Decide you want to heal. Some people can't let go of the pain, whether from a sense of misplaced loyalty, fear of living without it, or unwillingness to build a new future. Decide that whatever life you have left is still well worth living. Decide to look for joy. Decide to make each day as good as possible.

14. Make others smile. Give of yourself. Live in such a way that when you die, the world will be a better place because you lived.

Where Do I Turn? Recommended Books on Grief and Loss

Giving a good book is a highly effective way to offer grievers consolation, reliable advice, and solid information. They appreciate your thoughtfulness, especially if the book is closely matched to their own situation. Yet you do not have time to research the array of books that are available so you know what to give. We've done the work for you.

Here you find titles and descriptions of books about grief covering a range of styles and, although some overlap, we've organized them into situational categories. Some are recent, most were published within the last ten to fifteen years, and a few are old workhorses, published long ago but still well worth reading.

Often, newly bereaved people lack the concentration and desire to read long or complex books, so several listings consist of short chapters in easy-to-read formats. There are also more substantial books, for those who want information immediately or for those past the initial stages of grief who seek greater understanding.

We've noted when a book is spiritual or religious and where a clear denominational focus exists. In the absence of such comments, assume the book is secular in nature.

It's impossible to include every worthy book in this list. We base selections on our own reading, book reviews, personal experience, and over twenty-five years of working in the field of bereavement. Yet this list is fluid and changeable. You may wish to add to it yourself if you get other recommendations or read a book that is helpful.

If you need resources for a situation not listed here, or if you need more specific advice, please e-mail us at hello@corgenius.com.

Also, e-mail to let us know which books your friends and family find particularly pertinent or if you feel a book should be deleted from the list. We're always interested in the feedback of others whose experiences are different from ours so we can improve our offerings.

General Grief

Grieving Well: A Personal Journal for Adults about Loss by Judy Davidson. Center for Personal Recovery, 2002.

> The author was widowed at thirty and then survived the death of her oldest son when he was seventeen. As a grief educator and counselor, she skillfully created this interactive journal to help adults coping with the death of a loved one. Journaling is a well-established coping and healing mechanism, and Davidson's gentle leading questions make it comfortable to write about unresolved relationship issues, difficult days, positive memories, and new life.

> Recommended for any adult coping with the death of a loved one.

How to Survive the Loss of a Love by Peter McWilliams, Harold Bloomfield, and Melba Colgrove. Prelude Press, 1993.

> Grieving people are overwhelmed on many emotional and physical levels, and they appreciate smaller doses of information, support, and encouragement. This book is full of brief messages, including practical suggestions, proverbs, reminders, advice, and more. Readers can open the book randomly and find comfort on virtually every page.

> Recommended for anyone after death, divorce, estrangement, abandonment, or loss of a significant relationship.

Grief: What It Is and What You Can Do by Joy Johnson and Marvin Johnson. Centering Corp, 1995.

This inexpensive, small pamphlet contains user-friendly definitions and helpful hints. It is a brief, easy-to-read overview of grief appropriate for immediately after a death.

Recommended for people in the initial stages who would never tackle a whole book.

How to Go On Living When Someone You Love Dies by Therese Rando. Bantam, 1988.

Rando is a clinical psychologist and one of the most respected authors on bereavement for professional and personal audiences. She packed this book with well-researched information, advice, and resources for anyone who grieves. It is informative, compassionate, and down-to-earth.

Recommended for anyone grieving the death of a loved one, whether the death was last week or last year.

Living When a Loved One Has Died by Earl Grollman. Beacon Press, 1997.

The author wrote this longtime friend of the bereaved more than twenty years ago. This short book endures because it's easy to read and understand during the initial confusion of bereavement, yet it offers helpful words of comfort and guidance.

Recommended during the initial stages of grief or as an easy read at any point in the process.

What Helped Me When My Loved One Died by Earl Grollman. Beacon Press, 1982.

Rather than writing this book himself, Grollman assembled the stories of bereaved people and let them tell, in their own words, what helped them most when they were grieving. It is insightful and touching.

Recommended especially during the first six months to a year after a death and for those who live or work with bereaved people.

Swallowed by a Snake: The Gift of the Masculine Side of Healing by Thomas R. Golden. Golden Healing Publishing, 1996.

Much grief therapy is aimed toward the traditionally "feminine" tasks of reflection, relationships, and sharing of pain. Golden wrote this book to blend those tasks with the more traditionally "male" coping mechanisms of action, logic, and practicality. He found that both men and women have a blend of these characteristics, an insight that was confirmed by later research on grieving styles (referenced earlier in this guide).

This book, then, is a useful, balanced resource for any grieving adult.

Recommended for anyone who wants to understand our society's long-standing assumptions and be freed to grieve in his or her own style.

How We Grieve: Relearning the World by Thomas Attig. Oxford University Press, 2011.

The author recently revised this classic book, as he continues to draw on his thirty years of teaching and counseling. His core understanding is that grieving requires fundamentally "relearning the world" at every level. In this book, he offers rich stories, pertinent observations, and thoughtful reflections. His is a more objective look at grief that is well worth the read.

Recommended for anyone wanting to better understand the process of grief, whether they're currently grieving, anticipating a loss, or supporting a grieving person.

When Bad Things Happen to Good People by Harold Kushner. Schocken, 1981.

This Jewish rabbi writes for people of any Judeo-Christian faith tradition as he fearlessly addresses the dilemma created by the existence of suffering when God is supposed to be so good. This is a persuasive and hopeful examination of the empty platitudes often offered to the bereaved, and it poses a challenge to embrace the doubts, questions, and ambiguities of faith in the midst of crisis, death, and grief.

Recommended for those experiencing anger toward God or a faith crisis because of suffering or death.

Liberating Losses: When Death Brings Relief by Jennifer Elison and Chris McGonigle. Da Capo Press, 2004.

When a person dies, his or her loved one is expected to grieve. What happens if the primary emotion is relief? For instance, a dying loved one may be trapped in an increasingly debilitated body, and death is a longed-for release. Perhaps the person struggled with alcoholism or addiction and wreaked havoc in the family. Regardless of the cause, experiencing relief when someone dies is often a trigger for guilt. This honest yet compassionate book contains personal stories and case histories that validate the emotion most grieving people feel obliged to hide.

Recommended for "relieved grievers": those in circumstances where relief is a significant component of the grief process.

Coping with the Sudden Death of Your Loved One: Self-Help for Traumatic Bereavement by Therese Rando. Dog Ear Publishing, 2017.

Focusing on self-help strategies for mourners losing loved ones to sudden death, this book by an award-winning specialist in the field provides cutting-edge information and practical suggestions for dealing with the unique challenges posed by the volatile mixture of loss and trauma. The two largest sections of the text explain: a) the experience and unique trauma of sudden death, and b) how to develop a self-help plan to cope and heal. It is an excellent and up-to-date resource.

Highly recommended for anyone coping with sudden natural death, accident, disaster, suicide, or homicide.

I Wasn't Ready to Say Goodbye: Surviving, Coping, and Healing after the Sudden Death of a Loved One by Brook Noel and Pamela D. Blair. Champion Press, 2000.

Full of information for survivors of sudden death, this book begins by offering advice on calls to make, planning the service, and handling other immediate concerns. It goes on through the grief process, allowing for differences of age, gender, and relationship to the deceased.

Recommended any time from the initial notification of a sudden death through the grief process.

Grieving the Death of a Friend by Harold Ivan Smith. Augsburg Fortress, 1996.

Though these stories, quotes, and insights focus on close friendships and our society's denial of "friend grief," the wisdom they contain is helpful for anyone who grieves. The reflections begin with the dying process and continue through burying, mourning, remembering and reconciling. Finally, Smith includes rituals and suggestions for healing.

Recommended for anyone who grieves, but it is especially helpful during and after the death of a beloved person who wasn't an immediate family member.

Good Grief by Granger E. Westberg. Minneapolis: Fortress, 1997.

Originally written nearly forty years ago, this little book is still widely used. Westberg, drawing on extensive experience as a minister and counselor, demonstrates his belief that our response to smaller grief experiences affects our response to larger losses. He describes ten "stages" common to grief and shows how each one can bring growth and healing.

An old classic, recommended for anyone who grieves, particularly in the early stages when concentration is limited.

Understanding Your Grief: Ten Essential Touchstones for Finding Hope and Healing Your Heart by Alan D. Wolfelt. Companion Press, 2004.

The author, director of the Center for Loss and Life Transition, discusses factors that make grief unique for each person, describes what people normally think and feel during the grief process, and offers advice about how to get through it and heal. The book includes journaling sections that allow readers to formulate their thoughts in writing (a helpful strategy).

Recommended for those in any stage of the grief process

Living with Grief: After Sudden Loss, Suicide, Homicide, Accident, Heart Attack, Stroke by Kenneth J. Doka. Taylor and Francis, 1996.

Written by a preeminent researcher and therapist in the field of grief, this is an honest, valuable book for family members grieving sudden and unexpected death. In addition to the situations listed in the title, there is a helpful discussion of surviving the death of those in the military.

Recommended for those grieving a sudden, unexpected, or traumatic death, including military death.

Healing Your Grieving Heart after a Military Death: 100 Practical Ideas for Families and Friends by Bonnie Carroll and Alan Wolfelt. Companion Press, 2015.

Bonnie Carroll knows what she's talking about. She is a retired military officer, a bereaved military spouse, and the founder and president of TAPS (Tragedy Assistance Program for Survivors, a nonprofit organization dedicated to helping grieving families in the aftermath of a military death). She teamed up with a renowned grief counselor and educator to write this book focusing on the unique grief that follows a military death, whether as a result of hostile action, accident, illness, or suicide.

Recommended for military family members after a soldier dies, as well as those who wish to help support them.

Death of a Spouse

When Your Spouse Dies: A Widow & Widower's Handbook by Othniel J. Sieden and Jane L. Bilett. Books to Believe In, 2008.

The co-authors are a medical doctor who was widowed and a psychologist who eventually became his wife. They discuss financial issues and practical concerns while outlining an emotional road map to help guide widows and widowers as they heal and rebuild their lives.

Recommended for widowed people from the time of the death through the grief process.

When Your Spouse Dies: A Concise and Practical Source of Help and Advice by Cathleen L. Curry. Notre Dame: Ave Maria Press, 1990.

Widowed at the age of forty-seven with nine children to raise (her husband had a massive heart attack on the day before Father's Day), Curry incorporates her own experience and establishes eight practical guideposts for getting through the first year. She deals with topics ranging from expressions of mourning and caring for one's own health to loneliness, anger, sexuality, and financial planning. She emphasizes spiritual growth as essential to healing. This useful book is currently in its sixth printing.

Recommended for widowed persons, especially those who are younger and have children.

Widow to Widow: Thoughtful, Practical Ideas for Rebuilding Your Life by Genevieve Davis Ginsburg. Fisher Books, 1995.

Ginsburg is the founder of Widowed to Widowed Services, and she writes frankly and honestly about the needs, questions, and concerns of the widowed (men and women). She covers everything from empty-ing his or her closet, to traveling and eating alone, to money matters, to dating and sexuality. This is a wise, useful guide.

Recommended for any widowed person at any time.

Companion through the Darkness: Inner Dialogues on Grief by Stephanie Ericcson. HarperCollins, 1993.

The author began keeping a journal after her husband died while she was pregnant with their only child. She combines excerpts from that journal with brief essays, capturing the raw, wrenching depth of the emotions involved in grief.

Recommended for young widows, especially soon after the death.

Widowed by Joyce Brothers. Ballatine Publishing, 1990.

This is the personal story of a psychologist who thought she knew all there was to know about grieving a spouse's death until her own husband of thirty years died. It is wonderfully well written and serves as a comprehensive, down-to-earth, sometimes humorous, compas-sionate, and gentle look at the difficulties of negotiating the grief process as a widow.

Recommended for any widowed person.

Widower: When Men are Left Alone by Scott Campbell and Phyllis R. Silverman. Baywood, 1995.

A journalist and a behavioral scientist do a remarkable job of capturing the range of situations and emotions men feel when a wife dies. Each chapter centers on one widower. The authors give a brief biography and then allow the subject himself to tell his story and feelings in his own words. They follow this with well-done commentary grounded in research, pointing out aspects of each story that are important. It is a helpful, informative, and refreshing resource.

Recommended for men who are widowed.

I'm Grieving as Fast as I Can by Linda Feinberg. New Horizon Press, 1994.

Largely told through the stories of clients and friends combined with her own experience, Feinberg writes for young widows and widowers, often with small children. They immediately face issues of dating and sexuality, feel the burden of the family's needs, and struggle with the sense of a stolen or empty future. The author sensitively covers issues relating to a relationship that was stormy or abusive and even the loss of a fiancé.

Recommended for those under fifty who are widowed.

Finding Your Way after Your Spouse Dies by Marta Felber. Notre Dame: Ave Maria Press, 2000.

Having been through the experience, Felber offers sixty-four one-page essays on aspects of the grief process, from embracing loneliness, to reliving the day of the death, to dealing with guilt, and more. A brief Christian prayer and two scripture suggestions follow each essay. The book is practical, inspirational, honest, and easy to read.

Recommended for Christians who are widowed, especially those in the early stages of grief.

Parental Death—for Adults

Nobody's Child Anymore; Grieving, Caring, and Comforting When Parents Die by Barbara Bartocci. Notre Dame: Sorin Books, 2000.

Through nostalgia, a variety of stories, instruction, and inspiration, Bartocci captures the unique loss and life issues that accompany the death of a parent for an adult child. Unlike most grief books, she starts with the dying process and then goes on to issues of grieving, caring for the surviving parent, and healing from the loss. It is a wonderfully written, touching book, helpful to anyone who is grieving a parent's death.

Recommended from the time of a parent's terminal diagnosis through the death and grief.

How to Survive the Loss of a Parent: A Guide for Adults by Lois F. Akner. Morrow, 1993.

This book duplicates the setting of an actual ongoing workshop for adults whose parent(s) have died. There are twelve participants reflecting a range of ages, social and religious backgrounds, and family structure. In this informal format, the author (a psychotherapist) deftly guides the reader through the issues and emotions of parent loss in an accessible, sensible way.

Recommended for anyone whose parent dies.

When Parents Die: A Guide for Adults by Edward Myers. Penguin, 1997.

This book includes thoughtful advice from therapists, first-person accounts, and a detailed description of the author's own experience when each of his parents died. Myers knows how devastating a parent's death is, no matter how old you are. He covers the differences between sudden death and slow decline; gives advice for funerals, dividing property, and dealing with practical matters; and addresses resolving feelings of guilt, shame, and unfinished business.

Recommended from the time of a parent's diagnosis or death through the first six to nine months after the death.

Fatherloss: How Sons of All Ages Come to Terms with the Deaths of Their Dads by Neil Chethik. Hyperion, 2001.

This extraordinary book is based on a landmark national survey of more than 300 men whose fathers died plus extended interviews with seventy others. It details how men react differently to a father's death at ages ranging from childhood and young adulthood, to middle age and older, and then discusses what helps most.

Recommended highly for any man whose father died, even if the death was years ago.

On Grieving the Death of a Father by Harold Ivan Smith. Augsburg Fortress, 1994.

Smith is a prolific author on grief who intertwines his own experience with wisdom from the ages, such as Frederick Buechner, Norman Vincent Peale, Corrie ten Boom, and many other recognizable people. This easy read offers tidbits of wisdom to help heal without delving deeply into trauma.

Recommended soon after the death for middle-aged or older men whose father has died.

Grieving the Death of a Mother by Harold Ivan Smith. Augsburg Fortress, 2003.

The same author who almost ten years earlier wrote about the death of his father now writes an accessible and thorough book about the death of mothers. He describes his own experience but includes the experiences of many other people whose lives were deeply affected when their mother died. He begins his story with the dying process and continues through ways to remember and honor a mother long after her death.

Recommended for adult children from the time of their mother's terminal diagnosis through the grieving process.

Death of a Mother: Daughters' Stories edited by Rosa Ainley. HarperCollins, 1991.

This is a wonderful collection of more than thirty pieces written by women about the deaths of their mothers. Some are funny, others are filled with rage, some are despairing, and others are full of love. Well-known authors write some stories, while other authors are everyday women. The pieces include poetry, prose, reflection, and narrative.

Recommended for any woman whose mother has died.

Fatherless Women: How We Change After We Lose Our Dads by Clea Simon. John Wiley & Sons, 2001.

This highly acclaimed author and Boston Globe columnist fills her book with moving stories of real women combined with her own experience of her father's death. In some cases, the contributor's relationship with her father was enviable, and in others, it was conflicted. Regardless, each woman's thoughts contribute insights on making peace with the past and accepting the present, with a goal of moving into the future whole and healed.

Recommended for any woman whose father dies, regardless of the kind of relationship she had with him.

Motherless Daughters: the Legacy of Loss by Hope Edelman. Da Capo Press, 2006.

In this second edition, Edelman uses the experience of her mother's death when she was seventeen along with interviews of hundreds of other women whose mothers died, disappeared, or were otherwise lost from their lives. Combined with solid research, she explores the implications of yearning for the absent mother on a woman's self-concept, esteem, identity, and future relationships.

Recommended particularly for young adult women whose mother is absent through death, separation, or abandonment.

Child Death—for Parents

Help Your Marriage Survive the Death of a Child by Paul C. Rosenblatt. Philadelphia: Temple University Press, 2000.

A marriage requires hard work at the best of times. The impact of the death of a child can tear a family and marriage to shreds as the couple shuts down, turns away, or moves inward. Rosenblatt includes helpful information on how people grieve individually and in relationships; the impact of grief on sexuality; dealing with friends, relatives, and co-workers; the frequency of depression; and other important issues.

Recommended for couples at any time following a child's death.

Finding Life after Losing One by Nikki King and Alice Rampton. Cedar Fort, Inc., 2016.

Nikki King's toddler daughter died after her husband accidentally ran over her in their driveway. She joined with Alice Rampton, whose daughter died of an incurable illness, to write this profound book chronicling their experience as they cope with grief. Each chapter also includes excerpts from the stories of many other bereaved parents, broadening the scope of input.

Recommended for bereaved parents at any point in their grief journey.

Empty Cradle, Broken Heart: Surviving the Death of Your Baby by Deborah Davis. Fulcrum Publishing, 1991.

This is a wonderful, comforting book for parents grieving the death of a baby—miscarriage, stillborn, shortly after birth, or within the first year of life. The combination of personal narrative, research, and inspiration makes this a valuable resource. One unique aspect of the book is that it doesn't have to be read front to back; instead, it allows parents to choose topics specific to their situations.

Recommended in the initial stages of grief for any couple whose baby died before or shortly after birth.

A Child Dies: A Portrait of Family Grief by Joan Hagan Arnold and Penelope Buschman Gemma. The Charles Press, 1994.

Two nurses have written a comprehensive, invaluable resource for families struggling with the death of a child, whether it's an infant, a toddler, or an older child. The authors include powerful art and touching poetry along with practical advice from understanding companions.

Recommended for any couple or family grieving a child's death.

A Broken Heart Still Beats After Your Child Dies by Anne McCracken and Mary Semel. Hazelden, 1998.

This partnership of a social worker and a journalist, both of whom experienced the death of a child, results in a remarkable collection of poetry, fiction, and essays that indirectly but effectively capture the profound grief of parents when their child dies.

Recommended for parents any time after a still-at-home child dies.

Lament for a Son by Nicholas Westerhoff. Eerdmans, 1987.

In this powerfully written book, Wolterstorff (a professor of philosophical theology at Yale) grapples with questions, doubts, and family grief after his twenty-five-year-old son's death in a skiing accident. He incorporates philosophy, scripture, and poetry, and the afterword is a requiem written in memory of his son that was performed in Grand Rapids, Michigan.

Recommended for those with a slightly more academic or literary bent, especially within the first year.

Finding Your Way after Your Child Dies by Phyllis Vos Wezeman and Kenneth R. Wezeman. Ave Maria Press, 2001.

This book is a touching guide that helps parents acknowledge and deal with their feelings. It includes fifty-two themes, ranging from birthdays to graduation, and other events that may happen daily, weekly, or just once. Each theme includes a story or teaching about an aspect of grief, practical activities and rituals for coping, a reading from scripture, and a Christian prayer.

Recommended especially for Christian parents whose deceased child was under the age of eighteen.

When a Child Dies from Drugs: Practical Help for Parents in Bereavement by Patricia Wittberger and Russ Wittberger. Xlibris Corporation, 2004.

This book is by and for parents whose child dies from drugs or alcohol. It is also a useful guide for those who want to effectively support the grieving parents. It delves into the pain and stigma but also offers hope and practical advice.

Recommended for family and friends who survive a death caused by alcohol or drugs and for those who want to support them.

Five Cries of Grief: One Family's Journey to Healing After the Tragic Death of a Son by Merton Strommen and A. Irene Strommen. Minneapolis: Augsburg, 1996.

This couple chronicles their grief journey following their twenty-five-year-old son's death from a lightning strike. One unique aspect is that each author tells the story from their own perspective, highlighting the differences in each one's reactions and timetables and acknowledging the absolute necessity of accepting and dealing with those differences. They also reinforce the timeless aspect of grief and note that no magical healing occurs by the time of the anniversary.

Recommended for anyone in grief, but especially for couples and families grieving together.

Sibling Death

Surviving the Death of a Sibling: Living Through Grief When an Adult Brother or Sister Dies by T.J. Wray. Three Rivers Press, 2003.

This collection of stories by the author and many other sibling grievers is an excellent resource. The book is comforting, challenging, and inspiring while giving practical steps a grieving person can take to cope with a sibling's death.

Recommended for anyone over eighteen whose sibling dies.

When a Brother or Sister Dies: Looking Back, Moving Forward by Claire Berman. Praeger Publishers, 2009.

The author, whose adult sister died of a heart illness, takes an honest look at the fact that attention tends to focus on the grief of parents or children of the deceased rather than the grief of siblings. She admits the intense mix of emotions accompanying a sibling's death in light of the shared identity, intimate family history, and sometimes competitive or conflicted relationships that are common within families, and offers compassion and advice to survivors.

Recommended to adults surviving the death of a sibling.

Recovering From the Loss of a Sibling: When a Brother or Sister Dies by Katherine Fair Donnelly. Universe, 2000.

Numerous testimonials from surviving siblings of all ages form the foundation of this book. It addresses the unique grief of siblings and the fact that siblings are often overlooked in the outpouring of support for parents. The book is insightful and comforting.

Recommended for siblings from age ten to adult.

Losing Someone You Love: When a Brother or Sister Dies by Elizabeth Richter. Putnam, 1986.

This book consists of fifteen stories written by ten- to nineteen-year-olds whose brother or sister died. The cause of death varies widely: accidents, suicide, murder, disease, and even sudden infant death syndrome (SIDS). These honest stories let teens know they're not alone in their grief and that they will survive and heal.

Recommended for teens after a sibling dies.

Letters From a Friend: A Sibling's Guide for Coping and Grief by Erika R. Barber. Baywood, 2003.

This unique workbook includes therapeutic activities addressing the needs of children and adolescents after a sibling's death. It is organized into four sections: hospitalization, illness, injury, and death. Readers can easily remove pages to allow personalization of the text. This also allows independent use, so children and teens can create a personal journal of their bereavement and a chronicle of their lives as surviving siblings. It can be used by the entire family and/or in conjunction with a professional therapist.

Recommended for children or teens any time from a sibling's serious illness through death and the grieving process.

Books For and About Children or Teens

Straight Talk About Death for Teenagers: How to Cope with Losing Someone You Love by Earl A. Grollman. Boston: Beacon Press, 1994.

Earl Grollman has written more than twenty books on grief. This book uses an informal and accessible style to guide often-forgotten teenagers through the grieving process. Grollman doesn't go into depth on topics, and some may feel he glosses over too much. That is wise because teens aren't going to pick up a tome on grief. They will read this kind of introductory resource.

Recommended highly for teenagers who are grieving.

The Grieving Teen: A Guide for Teenagers and Their Friends by Helen Fitzgerald. Fireside, 2000.

In a clear, accessible way, Fitzgerald guides teens from the sickbed to the funeral, and from the first day back at school to the first anniversary of the death. She adeptly covers the entire range of situations for teen grief, helping them address the intense emotions they face as they deal with grief and adolescence simultaneously.

Recommended highly for teenagers coping with death.

Grief Skills for Life: A Personal Journal for Teens About Loss by Judy Davidson. Center for Personal Recovery, 2002.

Davidson is a death educator and trauma specialist whose oldest son died in a car accident at seventeen. This book is an interactive journal, inviting teens to write, draw, and color so they can laugh, cry, and release their emotions. It is cathartic, honest, and usable.

Recommended for any teen grieving a death.

A Child's Book About Death by Earl Grollman and Joy Johnson. Omaha: Centering Corporation, 2001.

> This is a brief, easy-to-read, comforting book for children when they face death. It explains death through analogy and experiences that children understand. Adults should spend time with it too.

> Recommended for parents and young children whenever death touches a family.

The Children Who Lived: Using Harry Potter and Other Fictional Characters to Help Grieving Children and Adolescents by Kathryn A. Markell and Marc A. Markell. Routledge, 2008.

> This sister and brother have written a creative, resourceful book that allows adults to use stories to help grieving kids and teens. Drawing from all seven Harry Potter stories plus four other classic works of fiction, the book talks about the loss issues they faced and then offers engaging projects, games, and activities to help youth strengthen their own coping skills. The book includes a CD that provides PowerPoint or JPEG formats for all the worksheets.

> Recommended for teachers, counselors, parents, and caregivers who are supporting grieving children.

Keys to Helping Children Deal with Death and Grief by Joy Johnson. Barron's Educational Press, 1999.

> Johnson relates her experiences as a bereavement specialist for over thirty years with a particular interest in children's grief. This book helps parents explain death in ways that kids can comprehend. It also explains a child's grief to parents in ways that allow them to understand and help. Stories and practical advice fill this invaluable, personal, and accessible guide.

> Recommended for parents and other adults helping children under the age of thirteen.

35 Ways to Help a Grieving Child by Dougy Center Staff. The Dougy Center for Grieving Children, 1999.

> Based on years of experience working directly with grieving kids, this guidebook is immensely practical and helpful. It covers topics

from how children of different ages grieve, to providing safe outlets for children to express their emotions, to involving kids in decisions that help them heal. Parents who work through this book with their children will benefit too.

Recommended as a workbook for parents and young to middle-aged children.

The Grieving Child: A Parent's Guide by Helen Fitzgerald. Simon & Schuster, 1992.

Organized like a book on infant care, this book provides practical advice for parents and others caring for bereaved children. The last chapter addresses the unresolved childhood grief that many adults carry and suggests how they can use the book to resolve their own grief while helping their children.

Recommended highly for parents of children from toddler to teenager.

Helping Children Grieve When Someone They Love Dies by Theresa M. Huntley. Minneapolis: Augsburg, 2002.

Huntley brings her energy and expertise as a pediatric nurse to this fine book to help parents (and other adults) to be more intentionally present with grieving children. This book inspires, educates, and motivates. The first and largest section of the book deals with information and advice to help children grieve the death of a loved one. The last third of the book covers how to help and support children who are dying.

Recommended for parents of dying or grieving children from youth through teen years.

Help Me Say Goodbye: Activities for Helping Kids Cope When a Special Person Dies by Janis Silverman. Fairview Press, 1999.

This little workbook is especially useful for younger children or any grieving children who have difficulty verbalizing their sadness and confusion. The child works through a series of activities, most of them nonverbal, to draw out their inner feelings. It can be equally helpful for the parents who work through it with them.

Recommended highly for young children and their parents.

Great Answers to Difficult Questions About Death: What Children Need to Know by Linda Goldman. Philadelphia: Jessica Kingsley, 2009.

Adults often wonder how to explain death to children. The author is a licensed counselor and teacher who uses simple sketches, discussion, quotes, questions, tasks, and connections to many resources in this useful guide. Chapters are devoted to religious beliefs, terminal illness, emotions, reactions of others, and the most common questions that kids ask.

Recommended for parents, teachers, youth ministers, and anyone who works with grieving children.

Sad Isn't Bad: A Good-Grief Guidebook for Kids Dealing with Loss by Michaelene Mundy. Abbey Press, 2006.

This is a helpful and hopeful workbook aimed at children in grades 1–3 that gives them images and language to describe their experience and guides them to recognize and cope with the losses in their lives in healthy ways. Parents and grandparents will benefit from working through the book with them.

Recommended for children in or close to the 4–8 age range who have to cope with loss.

Finding the Words: How to Talk with Children and Teens by Alan D. Wolfelt. Ft. Collins, CO: Companion Press, 2013.

The author offers a useful guide for parents, teachers, counselors and other adults who seek to offer support and comfort to children and adolescents dealing with "death, suicide, funerals, homicide, cremation, and other end-of-life matters." Introductory chapters address the uniqueness of children's grief, then ten chapters give helpful examples of possible language to use with different aged children (preschool to age 19) and different types of death or loss.

Recommended for anyone seeking to help children cope with death and illness.

Divorce

The Good Divorce: Keeping Your Family Together When Your Marriage Comes Apart by Constance Ahrons. N.Y: Harper Perennial, 1994.

The author interviewed ninety-eight families over a five-year period. Half of the couples were amicably divorced (cooperative colleagues and perfect pals), and half were enemies (fiery foes and angry associates). Ahrons challenges negative myths and stereotypes of divorce, providing a more accurate description based on the experience of real people. The best part of the book is the author's descriptions of the emotional divorce that precedes the legal divorce.

Recommended for anyone considering, going through, or completing a divorce.

Getting Divorced Without Ruining Your Life: A Reasoned, Practical Guide to the Legal, Emotional and Financial Ins and Outs of Negotiating a Divorce Settlement by Sam Margulies. NY: Fireside, 2001

The author is a lawyer and mediator with two decades of experience who gives extensive information about the legal, financial, and emotional dimensions of divorce. Partners are encouraged to collaborate rather than allow the process to be controlled by lawyers or an adversarial court system. Though by its nature the divorce process is emotionally charged, partners are repeatedly advised to feel but not act out their emotions, to keep their needs (and those of the children) in focus, to avoid being caught in the blame and victim role, and to take responsibility for ongoing choices.

Recommended for couples who have decided to divorce.

Adjusting to Divorce: Simple Steps Parents Can Take to Help Themselves and Their Children by Percy Ricketts. CreateSpace, 2009.

A psychotherapist and professor whose parenting classes are required for divorcing parents in the state of Florida, Dr. Ricketts highlights seven steps that help parents and their children adjust to the trauma and pain that occur with divorce.

Recommended for any divorcing family with children, especially children between the ages of five and eighteen.

Dumped: A Survival Guide for the Woman Who's Been Left by the Man She Loved by Sally Warren and Andrea Thompson. Avon, 1999.

> The authors draw on the experiences of over 100 women whose husbands left them, many times for another woman. The book is a down-to-earth, easy read with plenty of tips for daily survival (including how to answer the "What happened?" question) as well as long-term coping strategies. Warren went through the experience herself, and Thompson has written extensively for women's magazines. Their collaborative effort is one that many women find supportive and helpful.

> Recommended for women whose husbands left the marriage.

The Disenfranchised: Stories of Life and Grief When an Ex-Spouse Dies edited by Peggy Sapphire. Baywood, 2013.

> A counselor who has worked with divorced people extensively collected this anthology of stories. She noticed that, contrary to what many people expect, divorced people can experience profound grief when an ex-spouse dies. This unique resource addresses a common situation that often is not sufficiently validated.

> Recommended for divorced people when an ex-spouse dies.

Rebuilding When Your Relationship Ends by Bruce Fisher. San Luis: Impact, 2005.

> This is a wise, compassionate, and thorough exploration of nineteen building blocks that compose the divorce adjustment process. Each chapter ends with reflective questions and includes child adjustment considerations. Chapters are organized developmentally and include denial, fear, adaptation, loneliness, friendship, guilt/rejection, grief, anger, letting go, self-worth, transition, openness, love, trust, relatedness, sexuality, singleness, purpose, and freedom.

> Recommended highly for anyone going through and adjusting to divorce.

Terminal Illness

Final Gifts: Understanding the Special Awareness, Needs, and Communications of the Dying by Maggie Callanan and Patricia Kelley. Simon and Schuster, 2012. (Updated from the 1997 version)

This book ought to be on every shelf. In clear and simple terms, these two hospice nurses tell story after story to illustrate the ways we can understand what loved ones experience as they die. It lets family members truly communicate with their dying loved one, finish unfinished business, and help achieve the kind of peaceful death everyone hopes to have.

Recommended for anyone with aging parents, family members who are frequently ill, the family of a terminally ill patient, and all those wanting to make the death process easier for everyone involved.

When the Dying Speak by Ron Wooten-Green. Loyola Press, 2001

The author is a hospice chaplain, a former university professor, and a widower himself. Drawing on his personal and ministerial experiences and writing from a Christian perspective, he uses each chapter to explain elements of communicating with dying people and then concludes with reflection questions for the reader.

Recommended for people from Christian faith traditions who want to be truly present during the dying process of a beloved person.

Healing a Friend or Loved One's Grieving Heart after A Cancer Diagnosis: 100 Practical Ideas for Providing Compassion, Comfort, and Care by Alan D. Wolfelt and Kirby J. Duvall. Ft. Collins, CO: Companion Press, 2014.

Wolfelt and his co-author have again teamed up, this time focused on responding to someone who is coping with cancer. Wolfelt describes the many types of loss involved in cancer diagnosis and treatment, even if the treatment is successful. Then they give practical ideas paired with a meaningful quote and a closing suggestion for a helpful thought, action, or companionship activity.

Recommended for anyone who cares about a person with a serious cancer diagnosis.

Being Mortal: Medicine and What Matters in the End by Atul Gawandi. Metropolitan Books, 2014.

This highly respected doctor is the author of several bestselling books about medicine and healthcare. This award-winning book is an honest look at the goals and limits of modern medicine, especially as people age and die.

Recommended for anyone who wishes to better understand the decisions and implications of treatments for serious or terminal illness.

When Breath Becomes Air by Paul Kalanithi. Random House, 2016.

A beautifully written memoir by a young doctor who unexpectedly receives a diagnosis of stage IV lung cancer, this compelling book describes his thoughts and fears, his wife's and family's reactions, and what it's like to face the certainty of a much shorter life than he had planned.

Recommended for those wishing to explore the experience, feelings, and thoughts of a terminally ill man and his family.

Dementia

Understanding Memory Loss: Loss: What to Do When You Have Trouble Remembering. National Institute on Aging.

This free government resource is an invaluable educational tool covering sources of forgetfulness and essential knowledge about dementia. It is available in printable PDF form or for ordering at http://www.nia.nih.gov/alzheimers/publication/understanding-memory-loss.

Recommended for everyone before there are signs of dementia so they understand signs and causes.

Caring for a Person with Alzheimer's Disease. National Institute on Aging.

A more substantial free government booklet, this piece focuses on how a family can best support and access services for someone diagnosed with Alzheimer's. It is available in printable PDF form or for ordering at http://www.nia.nih.gov/alzheimers/publication/caring-for-a-person-with-alzheimers-disease

Recommended for family and caregivers of anyone diagnosed with Alzheimer's disease or other sources of dementia.

Loving Someone Who Has Dementia: How to Find Hope While Coping with Stress and Grief by Pauline Boss. Jossey-Bass, 2011.

This book isn't so much about the person who has dementia; instead, it's about the caregivers and family members. The author is a therapist

192 | AMY FLORIAN

who also worked as a professor at the University of Minnesota and at Harvard Medical School. She sensitively discusses how relationships change as dementia progresses and offers seven guidelines to help caregivers keep their sanity. This is a great resource.

Recommended for the family members, friends, and other concerned people who are dealing with the progressing dementia of a loved one.

Alzheimer's Disease and Other Dementias: The Caregiver's Complete Survival Guide by Nataly Rubinstein. Two Harbors Press, 2011.

The author is a licensed clinical social worker and certified geriatric care manager specializing in dementia. She worked with dementia patients for two decades and served as her mother's caregiver for sixteen years as her dementia progressed. She draws on her experience of what works and what doesn't, especially in common problem areas, to offer eminently practical, how-to tips for the family members and caregivers. Having navigated the system repeatedly on behalf of others, she includes tips on getting the legal, financial, and medical help you and your loved one need along with a wealth of other information.

Recommended for anyone concerned about or caring for a person with dementia.

The 36-Hour Day: A Family Guide to Caring for People Who Have Alzheimer Disease, Related Dementias, and Memory Loss by Nancy L. Mace and Peter V. Rabins. John Hopkins University Press, 2011.

Originally published by Johns Hopkins in 1981, this book has been continually revised, updated, and improved and is now in its fifth edition. A valuable and comprehensive manual recommended by the Journal of the American Medical Association, the book covers issues from the causes and prevention of dementia, through handling the early stages, and on to finding appropriate care that manages more advanced dementia.

Recommended as an educational resource for anyone seeking education while facing the possibility or reality of dementia.

Learning to Speak Alzheimer's: A Groundbreaking Approach for Everyone Dealing with the Disease by Joanne Koenig Coste. Mariner Books, 2004.

The author is an Alzheimer's family therapist and board member of the *American Journal of Alzheimer's Disease & Other Dementias* who raised four children while caring for her husband following his stroke and progressive memory loss. She developed a process she calls "habilitation" to enhance the person's remaining functions while compensating for what they have lost and to improve the level of communication between all concerned. She doesn't offer education about the illness itself and assumes a full-time caregiver relationship. In that context, she offers useful advice and tips on a wide range of issues (e.g., recipes for nutritious finger foods and helping the person get a good night's sleep). This is a highly regarded source of information from a nationally recognized expert.

Recommended for people who want input on emotional and personal aspects of caring for their loved one with dementia, particularly if they are full-time caregivers.

Depression and Anxiety in Later Life: What Everyone Needs to Know by Mark D. Miller and Charles F. Reynolds III. Johns Hopkins Press, 2012.

Millions of elderly people struggle with depression and anxiety, often complicated by memory problems, health issues, physical pain, difficulty eating or sleeping, and end-of-life fears. This book delves into the causes, symptoms, and treatments of mental disorders in older people. The aim is to help the elderly, their family members, and caregivers identify symptoms and make positive lifestyle changes to help the "golden years" have a little more luster.

Recommended for aging people, their adult children, and caregivers.

Where Two Worlds Touch: A Spiritual Journey Through Alzheimer's Disease by Jade Angelica. Skinner House, 2014.

This sensitively-written, practical road map mixes Christian spirituality with supremely practical instructions for every step of Alzheimer's disease. The author, who also founded Healing Moments to provide creative strategies to Alzheimer's caregivers across the country, emphasizes the value and beauty of the person affected, focusing more on what can still be done than what is lost. It is helpful, hopeful, comforting, and extremely usable.

Recommended for Alzheimer's caregivers, especially if they have a Christian perspective.

Death by Suicide

No Time to Say Goodbye: Surviving the Suicide of a Loved One by Carla Fine. Three Rivers Press, 1999; Kindle, 2011

> The author's husband of twenty-one years was a successful physician at the top of his game when he killed himself. Feeling stunned, stigmatized, guilty, isolated, and at a loss for resources, she wrote this comprehensive manual for those surviving a loved one's suicide. In an honest, sometimes raw, insightful, and eminently practical way, she covers the emotional, legal, financial, and psychological effects as survivors struggle to make sense of the death and grow beyond it.

> Recommended for adults whose spouse, relative, or close friend died by suicide.

My Son . . . My Son: A Guide to Healing After Death, Loss, or Suicide by Iris Bolton. Atlanta: Iris Bolton Press, 1983.

> This moving and powerful book is still considered the best on child or adolescent suicide. Bolton compassionately and clearly covers the emotional, physical, and psychological devastation, including the denial, the lack of knowledge about suicide, and the despair common to survivors. She helps the family cope and come to a point of resolution and peace.

> Recommended highly for any family surviving the suicide of a child.

A Long-Shadowed Grief: Suicide and Its Aftermath by Harold Ivan Smith. Cowley Publications, 2007.

> This compassionate, serious discussion includes managing guilt, dealing with other people, finding spirituality, losing naiveté, and learning to go on.

> An excellent resource for anyone who has experienced a death by suicide.

But I Didn't Say Goodbye: For Parents and Professionals Helping Child Suicide Survivors by Barbara Rubel. GriefCenter, 2000.

> This story of a child survivor and the adults in his life helps children deal with the difficulties and the stigmatizing aftermath of suicide.

The end of each chapter includes worksheets and exercises that can help both parent and child if they complete them together.

Recommended for parents and other adults helping a child affected by suicide.

But I Didn't Say Goodbye: Helping Children and Families After a Suicide by Barbara Rubel. 2nd edition. Kendall Park, NJ: Griefwork Center, Inc. 2009.

Barbara Rubel's second book on suicide builds upon her first book and, rather than being aimed at parents and professionals, is more specifically aimed at children and families. As the numbers of suicides increase, including more girls, older adults, and post-traumatic stress disorder (PTSD) veterans, this book's format of a conversational workbook is helpful.

Recommended for family and friends, first responders, clergy, counselors, and anyone affected by suicide.

History of a Suicide: My Sister's Unfinished Life by Jill Bialosky. Atria, 2011.

Kim was a beautiful, tenderhearted twenty-one-year-old when she took her own life. Her half-sister Jill was heartbroken and haunted by Kim's inexplicable decision. She took nearly twenty years to process the questions, conduct research on suicide in young people, and create this invaluable memoir that combines science, psychology, and the agony of surviving a loved one's suicide. It is honest, riveting, authentic, and eminently useful.

Recommended for family, friends, and loved ones before and/or after a suicide.

The Suicidal Mind by Edwin S. Shneidman. Oxford University Press, 1998.

This classic book remains the best means to understand the underlying processes and thoughts of a suicidal person. It is a somewhat academic book written by the groundbreaking researcher in the area of suicide, but it's accessible to everyone. He describes five clusters into which most suicides fall and ten psychological commonalities among suicides.

Recommended for those who want to undertake a serious investigation of the causes and underlying factors behind suicide.

Seeking Hope: Stories of the Suicide Bereaved by Michelle Linn-Gust and Julie Cerel. Chellehead Works, 2011.

> Every time a person dies by suicide, family and friends are left behind to grieve, regret, wonder, and cope. This is a helpful collection of first-person stories written by loved ones after a suicide. They are honest accounts that illustrate the complicated grief and stigma that follows suicide but also offer hope and healing for survivors.

> Recommended for anyone affected by a suicide.

In Her Wake: A Child Psychiatrist Explores the Mystery of Her Mother's Suicide by Nancy Rappaport. NY: Basic Book, 2009.

> The author's mother died by suicide when she was a young child. She lived with a haunting shadow surrounding her mother's death, where the suicide seemed to form the definition of her mother and colored everything about her memories. In this scientifically-grounded but compassionate book, she puts a proper face on the stigma and aftermath of suicide, and gives practical strategies for redeeming the person's life, significance, and memory.

> Recommended for anyone surviving a loved one's suicide death, even if it has been years.

Murder or Violence

A Grief Like No Other: Surviving the Violent Death of Someone You Love by Kathleen O'Hara. Marlowe and Company, 2006.

> The author is a licensed therapist who has counseled hundreds of grieving people. When her own son was brutally murdered, she developed these concrete, practical steps to help guide the family and friends of a murder victim through the complicated vortex of grief that follows violent death.

> Recommended for survivors of a murder, victim service providers, and friends.

Homicide Survivors: Misunderstood Grievers by Judie A. Bucholz. Baywood, 2002.

> The author is a murder victim survivor who collected stories of families that have faced this terrible tragedy. It follows survivors

through court trials and publicity, the emotional roller coaster, and the awkwardness of conversations with others. The book provides a compassionate, honest look at the complicated grief process on personal and social levels.

Recommended for survivors of a murder and those who wish to companion them.

No Time for Goodbyes: Coping with Sorrow, Anger and Injustice After a Tragic Death by Janice Harris Lord. Bargo, 1991.

Lord, a death educator and grief counselor, has written an invaluable aid to those whose loved ones were murdered, killed by a drunk driver, or died in other violent and tragic circumstances. Lord deals with the possibility of trials, public attention, shock, denial, and all of the intense emotions that swirl through a family struck by sudden, violent death.

Recommended for families dealing with violent death.

A Terrible Thing Happened: A Story for Children Who Have Witnessed Violence or Trauma by Margaret M. Holmes. Magination Press, 2000.

This sensitive book tells the story of Sherman Smith, who saw a terrible thing happen. The "thing" is never named, allowing children to insert their own experience as they walk through Sherman's tale. He tries at first to forget or ignore it, but that makes him feel funny and have bad dreams. He only feels better when he meets someone who helps him talk about the terrible thing.

Recommended for adults who live or work with young children who witness abuse, murder, suicide, an accident, or another traumatic experience.

Pet Death

The Loss of a Pet by Wallace Sife. Howell Book House, 3rd edition, 2005.

The founder of the Association for Pet Bereavement writes a wide-ranging but concise book detailing the grief a pet owner feels when his or her beloved companion dies or has to be given up due to circumstances beyond anyone's control. He recognizes the special bond older people form with their pets, especially if they're single, and the special attachment of children to animals. He discusses euthanizing pets, including whether to stay with the pet until the last breath, and he covers the stages of pet grief, techniques for dealing with anger, recognizing deeper problems that are masked by mourning, pet cemeteries, and the impact of religious beliefs (with articles by a number of religious leaders). This is the most comprehensive book available for the death or loss of a pet.

Highly recommended for any adult who loves a pet.

Saying Good-Bye to the Pet You Love: A Complete Resource to Help You Heal by Lorri A. Greene. New Harbinger, 2002.

The author is a psychologist recognized for her expertise in pet grief. She writes in practical but compassionate terms about the often-misunderstood feelings people have after the pet they love dies. She discusses the importance of the human-animal bond and offers strategies for working through the grief process.

Recommended for any adult whose pet died.

When a Family Pet Dies: A Guide to Dealing with Children's Loss by JoAnn Tuzeo-Jarolmen. Kingsley, 2006.

This is an easy-to-read, comprehensive guide for understanding a child's grief when a beloved family pet dies. The author discusses age-based comprehension, whether or when to get a new pet, and how to address the child's emotional needs in ways that help him or her move on.

Recommended for parents after the death of a family pet.

Conclusion

In this book, we face the issues that make most people terribly uncomfortable. We name realities we don't want to face. We teach lessons that are learned best in the crucible of pain.

Why would you choose to read such a book? There is one fundamental reason: Life is an hourglass, and it is stuck to the table. None of us knows how many grains of sand we have left in the top, and none of us can stop the last grain of sand from going through to the bottom. We are not in control, and life can be forever changed in the flash of an instant.

While you still have sand remaining in your hourglass, every single grain is precious. Life is more vibrant when you are aware of the gift in each moment. You take less for granted when you acknowledge that you do not truly "own" anything, for it can all disappear tomorrow. You live with more kindness, tolerance, perspective, and gratitude when you realize you don't know how long you will have the people you love. You help others heal and regain joy when you know how to effectively companion them through the toughest times of life. Awareness of the fragility and tenuous nature of life provides meaning you cannot gain any other way.

I hope you have the courage to face these difficult topics. I hope you choose to live as fully as possible until you take your last breath and help others to do the same. Use these lessons to make the most of every single grain of sand in the hourglass of your life.

Thank you for spending a few of those precious grains with me.

Keep In Touch

I'd love to hear your stories, questions, and input. Tell what works best for you or what you learned that made a difference. Tell what else you'd like to know, so I can include it in the next edition of this book.

E-mail hello@corgenius.com or call us at 847-882-3491. We're committed to doing whatever we can to help you walk yourself and your loved ones through the toughest times of life. Dare to make a difference. You will never regret it.

We look forward to hearing from you.

Bibliography
of Resources Used

Anna Nalick's song "Breathe" contains the lyrics, "And life's like an hourglass, glued to the table." We are indebted to Anna for that inspiration.

Attig, Thomas. *How We Grieve: Relearning the World*. Oxford University Press, 2011.

Boss, Pauline. *Ambiguous Loss: Learning to Live with Unresolved Grief*. Harvard University Press, 1999.

Bridges, William. *Making Sense of Life's Changes*. Da Capo Press, 2004.

Byock, Ira. *The Four Things That Matter Most: A Book About Living*. Free Press, 2004.

Byock, Ira. *The Best Care Possible: A Physician's Quest to Transform Care Through the End of Life*. Avery, 2012.

Callanan, Maggie and Patricia Kelley. *Final Gifts: Understanding the Special Awareness, Needs, and Communications of the Dying*. Simon & Schuster, 2012.

Chochinov, Harvey M., Linda J. Krisjanson, Thomas F. Hack, Tom Hassard, Susan McClement, and Mike Harlos. "Dignity in the Terminally Ill: Revisited." *Journal of Palliative Medicine*. Vol. 9 No. 3, June 2006. 666–672.

Corr, Charles A. and Donna M. Corr. *Death and Dying, Life and Living*. 7th edition. Wadsworth Publishing, 2012.

DeSpelder, Lynne Ann and Albert Lee Strickland. *The Last Dance: Encountering Death and Dying*. McGraw-Hill, 2008.

Doka, Kenneth J. and Terry L. Martin. *Grieving Beyond Gender: Understanding the Ways Men and Women Mourn*. Taylor & Francis, 2010.

Doka, Kenneth J. *Living with Grief: After Sudden Loss, Suicide, Homicide, Accident, Heart Attack, Stroke*. Taylor & Francis, 1996.

Doka, Kenneth J. *Disenfranchised Grief: Recognizing Hidden Sorrow*. Lexington Books, 1989.

Goldman, Marlene B. and Maureen C. Hatch. *Women & Health*. Academic Press, 2000.

Jordan, John R. and John L. McIntosh. *Grief After Suicide: Understanding the Consequences and Caring for the Survivors*. Routledge, 2010.

Kessler, David. *The Needs of the Dying: A Guide for Bringing Hope, Comfort, and Love to Life's Final Chapter*. Harper Collins, 1997.

Meager, David K. and David E. Balk (eds.). *Handbook of Thanatology: The Essential Body of Knowledge for the Study of Death, Dying, and Bereavement*. Routledge, 2007.

Miller, Mark D. and Charles F. Reynolds III. *Depression and Anxiety in Later Life: What Everyone Needs to Know*. Johns Hopkins Press, 2012.

Mitchell, Kenneth R. and Herbert Anderson. *All Our Losses, All Our Griefs: Resources for Pastoral Care*. Westminster John Knox Press, 1983.

Morris, Virginia. *Talking About Death Won't Kill You*. Workman Publishing, 2001.

Neimeyer, Robert A. (ed.) *Meaning Reconstruction and the Experience of Loss*. American Psychological Association, 2001.

Ramirez, Gerardo and Sian L. Beilock. "Writing About Testing Worries Boosts Exam Performance in the Classroom." *Science*, Vol. 331 No. 6014, 2011. 211–213.

Rando, Therese A. (ed.) *Clinical Dimensions of Anticipatory Mourning: Theory and Practice in Working with the Dying, Their Loved Ones, and Their Caregivers*. Research Press, 2000.

Rando, Therese A. *Grief and Mourning: Accommodating to Loss*. In Hannelore Wass & Robert A. Neimeyer (eds.), Dying: *Facing the Facts*. 3rd edition. Taylor and Francis, 1995.

Spencer, Sabina A. and John D. Adams. *Life Changes: A Guide to the Seven Stages of Personal Growth*. Paraview Press, 2002.

Stroebe, Margaret, Henk Schut, and Jan van den Bout (eds.). *Complicated Grief: Scientific Foundations for Health Care Professionals*. Routledge, 2012.

Stroebe, Margaret and Henk Schut. "The Dual Process Model of Coping with Bereavement: Rationale and Description." *Death Studies*. Vol. 23 No. 3, 1999. 197–224.

Werth, James L. and Laura Crow. "End-of-Life Care: An Overview for Professional Counselors." *Journal of Counseling and Development*. Vol. 87 No. 2, 2009. 194–202.

Winokuer, Howard R. and Darcy L. Harris. *Principles and Practice of Grief Counseling*. Springer Publishing, 2012.

Worden, William. *Children and Grief: When a Parent Dies*. The Guilford Press, 2001.

Worden, William. Grief Counseling and Grief Therapy, 4th edition. Springer Publishing, 2008.

About the Author

The most formative experience in Amy Florian's life occurred when her husband died in a car accident at the age of twenty-five, leaving her a widow with a seven-month-old son. She subsequently dedicated herself to teaching about transition, death, and grief, so others could learn how to effectively companion people through the toughest times of life.

Amy holds a master's degree and is a Fellow in Thanatology (the highest level of certification through the Association for Death Education and Counseling, achieved by fewer than 200 people in the United States). Amy worked with more than 2,000 grieving people over the past twenty-five years. She taught graduate and undergraduate courses at universities in the Chicago area, and facilitates an ongoing support group for widowed persons that she helped found in 1988. She has published more than one hundred articles and is internationally recognized as a unique, inspirational, and powerful presenter at conferences and seminars. The depth of her knowledge and experience is exceeded only by her passion, which shows through in everything she does.

Manufactured by Amazon.ca
Bolton, ON

11803578R00122